Restoring the Soul

Living Free from the
Wounds and Hurts of Life

Geoff Wattoff
D. Min.
January 2023

Published by Timothy Publishing Services
3409 W Gary St.
Broken Arrow, OK 74012
918-924-6246

Library of Congress Control Number: 2023902657

Text Design: Lisa Simpson

ENDORSEMENTS

Dr. Geoff Wattoff presents a balanced biblical, historical, and experiential approach to inner healing. He does not speak merely academically, but personally from his own experience of receiving inner healing as well as his years of ministry experience leading others to freedom through inner healing. We have partnered together well as a team to set people free. Dr. Wattoff builds upon a biblical foundation, providing historical support, and interweaves credible case studies of inner healing. He candidly shares real life traumas healed by the power of Christ within. I highly recommend *Restoring the Soul* and the ministry of Dr. Wattoff.

Paul L. King, Th.D., D.Min.
Pastor, Professor, President of Paul King Ministries, Inc.,
Author of 15 books, including God's Healing Arsenal

Dr. Geoff Wattoff teaches Inner Healing at Global Awakening Theological Seminary. I am the one who recruited him. After you read this book, you will know why. His approach to inner healing focuses on bringing the light of the truth of the Word of God to dispel the darkness of lies we have believed, to free us from fear, and to heal wounds caused by others or were self-inflicted. This book presents a way to freedom—freedom to become the person God created us to be—equipped to do the work of his Kingdom. Dr. Wattoff shares his wisdom of inner healing with keen wit and an engaging sense of humor.

Dr. Tom Litteer, Assistant Dean,
Global Awakening Theological Seminary

Dr. Geoffrey Wattoff, through the inspiration and direction of the Holy Spirit, has given the Body of Christ a precious gift in writing *Restoring the Soul*. It is a rare treasure to find a book that treats God's promises regarding inner healing—freedom of the soul—with extensive scriptural depth and accuracy while still having the readability to reach an audience at every level. This book is both for the one seeking to live free as well as the one helping another gain freedom. Biblical insights as well as stories of this author's personal journey lets the reader see God's compassion and desire for His children to live in the liberty we have in Jesus. Thank you, Dr. Wattoff, for this work of love for God's people.

Eva Benevento, D.Min
Author of Power of Touch and
Covenants and Pinky Promises

Geoff's book spoke straight to me. It is extremely clear and easy to read. This book is a helpful balance of content, and pertinent stories. It is practical, and concise. This book was for me a wisdom tune-up where Geoff adjusted the motor and aligned the wheels that run my heart. He marvelously weaves together principles and stories making the book accessible and easy to use.

Gerard Labrecque, D. Min., Dream Coach

Restoring the Soul is a must read for all looking for healing of emotional and spiritual wounds. It is also valuable for those who seek to lead others into greater spiritual maturity and power. Dr. Geoff Wattoff's knowledge of the Word of God coupled with his humor and relatability make his wisdom accessible to all. *Restoring the Soul* blends Dr. Wattoff's understanding of inner healing with Scripture to demonstrate that God's people can walk in wholeness and freedom. This book is for the beginner who is seeking to understand inner healing as well as the seasoned Christian looking for greater insight and understanding.

J.J. Jennings, Pastor Woodlake Family Church Turley

TABLE OF CONTENTS

DEDICATION

In memory of Kris Mineau
A man who modeled what it is to live a godly life with integrity

ACKNOWLEDGMENTS

Many years ago, I had no interest in inner healing. That I have been teaching it for several years at a seminary and publishing a book on the subject is a testimony to the grace of God and the help and support of many people, including:

Dr. Tom Litteer, Assistant Dean at GATS (Global Awakening Theological Seminary). We have spent countless hours over the last several years at Einstein's Bagels discussing everything from inner healing to theology to golf club design. Without your friendship, insight, and encouragement, this book would not exist.

Genevieve Chartrand a constant source of encouragement and help. You continually motivate me to be better.

Ben and Eva Benevento, who have been friends to my wife Joanie and me for many years. I am especially grateful to Ben for his prophetic insight and encouragement and to Eva for her tireless help in transforming my initial draft into something readable.

The ministry of Global Awakening. I'm honored to be part of this incredible ministry and to have the opportunity to draft in your wake.

My Woodlake Church family, especially J.J. and Jennifer Jennings, pastors of Woodlake Turley.

To my three children, Joshua, Jennifer, Elizabeth, and my sons-in-law Ian and Chris, for their love and support.

And most importantly, to Joanie, my wife of over forty-four years. You have stood by my side, encouraged, loved, and believed in me when I didn't. You are the greatest gift God has given me.

FOREWORD

The ministry of Inner Healing is about freedom—freedom to live fully for God unencumbered by our own self-absorption, deception by the powers of darkness, and the emotional and spiritual wounds of the past. God has made a way for our redemption, our healing, and our restoration to health and wholeness through the power of the cross and the resurrection of our Lord Jesus, the Great Physician.

Dr. Geoff Wattoff, who teaches Inner Healing at Global Awakening Theological Seminary, offers his book *Restoring the Soul* as a means by which anyone may, through the ministry of the Holy Spirit, embrace this promise of Jesus, "The thief comes only to steal, kill, and destroy, but I came that you may have life and have it abundantly" (John 10:10). In this abundant life, we experience what Dr. Wattoff describes as becoming "free of the fear of man and the fear of failure...fully living out your life as God intended." He and his wife Joanie have ministered to hundreds of people, personally witnessing God's power to set his sons and daughters free.

Dr. Wattoff clearly states that this is not a book of theories—and it isn't. He has provided a book of practical methods based on the Word of God and gleaned from years of study and application. You can be certain that you will find help here in becoming all that God meant for you to be—a beloved child of the King of Heaven whose heart has been cleansed and mind renewed, now able to hear God's voice and know the purpose for which you have been created.

Know that God has not forgotten you and no matter where you have been, where you are now, or what sorrows you have endured, there is nothing too hard for the One who loves you and wants you to be free. Dr. Wattoff's book will encourage you and set you on a pathway to a brand new beginning. I highly recommend it and Dr. Wattoff. I remember how my eyes were opened to such great truths to set one free when I read my first book on inner healing in 1984. May your eyes be opened to these truths in this book for our times.

Dr. Randy Clark, D.D., D.Min., Th.D.,
Overseer of the apostolic network of Global Awakening
President of Global Awakening Theological Seminary

INTRODUCTION

"Cages" — We the Kingdom

What if I got real honest?
What if I took a risk?
What if I opened up my heart
And let you see in?
What if I took my mask off?
Trying to fit in
I don't wanna be a mannequin
What if I let my guard down?
What if I took a breath?
What if I wasn't perfect?
What if I was just a mess?
What if I bled my soul out
Givin' all I could give?
I'm so tired of pretending
I'm comin' out of my cages
I'm steppin' down from my stages
I'm sick and tired of faking it
What I wouldn't give to be known[1]

Take a few minutes and ponder these lyrics. This song is about throwing off the shackles, getting rid of the façade, and living an authentic life as the person God created each of us to be. I believe deep in the heart of every individual is a desire to experience the message in this song. What if we could break off all of the shackles that have held us down? What if we could shed the false expectations of others? What if we could live free from the fear of man, the fear of failure?

---

[1] Andrew Bergthold, Franni Cash, Scott Mctyeire Cash, Edward Martin Cash, Edmond Martin Jr Cash, Kyle Reed Briskin. "Cages," in *Holy Water,* (Brentwood, TN: Sparrow 2020).

The book you are reading is designed to help you on a guided journey toward authenticity. A journey where you will discover, maybe for the first time, who you really are. A journey where you will step into the place where you are fully living your life as God, not anybody else, intended.

On this journey, you will learn what it's like to be loved and free. You will discover your uniqueness as a man or as a woman of God. This is an opportunity to truly experience God's joy, peace, and love in your daily existence.

You are embarking on a road to freedom, to authenticity. Only when we are our authentic selves can we experience the freedom Jesus died to give us. Along the way, you will identify the lies, the fears, and the wounds that have kept you bound. At times identifying and shedding them will be painful, but it will be worth it. The process may, at times, feel like major surgery. I've had a few surgeries, and the first few days following the surgery were the most painful. Eventually, the pain subsided, and I was healthier than before the surgery. None of the surgeries were fun, but they were all worth it.

Some of you may be excited about this journey. Some of you may be entering into this with fear and trepidation. Regardless, at the end of the road, there is freedom.

How can I be so sure that you can find freedom? That sounds like a bold, almost arrogant claim. I can be sure because I know the God who will walk down this road with you. I know his heart, his love, his compassion. The Lord Jesus suffered on the cross, taking our sin and shame upon himself. He suffered, paying the ultimate price for one reason; so that we could be reconciled to God, Father, Son, and Holy Spirit, and experience true freedom. The Bible declares,

For while we were still helpless, at the right time, Christ died for the ungodly. For rarely will someone die for a just person—though for a good person perhaps someone might even dare to die. But God proves his own love for us in that while we were still sinners, Christ died for us. How much more then, since we have now been justified by his blood, will we be saved through him from wrath. For if, while we were enemies, we were reconciled to God through the death of his Son, then how much more, having been reconciled, will we be saved by his life. And not only that, but we also boast in God through our Lord Jesus Christ, through whom we have now received this reconciliation. (Rom 5:6-11)

Jesus didn't come because we were good; he came because we were helpless. He knew our depraved sinful condition, yet he loved us enough to pay the price we owed but couldn't pay. Our salvation, our conversion, didn't end there. Jesus came to set us free. He is still working in us, helping us live free. Jesus came to "proclaim release to the captives, and recovery of sight to the blind, to set free the oppressed" (Luke 4:18). The freedom many of us desperately seek was purchased for us by Jesus on the cross (Isa 53:4-5, Isa 61:1).

This book is not a book of theories. My wife and I have seen hundreds of people set free from all kinds of bondage. Nothing is too hard for our God. The principles in this book are those that we have used in helping others find freedom. They have been tested. They work because they are principles established by God, meaning they are eternal and unchanging. Take your time going through the material. I am firmly convinced that as you learn to apply the truths presented here, you will find the freedom you seek.

My prayer for you —

Father, I come to you on behalf of the man, the woman reading this book. Father, I am asking that your love, your presence would be real to them as they read this. Father, I thank you that you are committed to their freedom. Open their eyes and let them see who you created them to be. Holy Spirit, I am asking you to identify the lies, the wounds, and the root issues in their lives that have held them back. Give them the courage to leave those things behind. Grant them the grace to forgive those who have hurt them. Give them the grace to forgive themselves. Let them remove the cloak of shame they have been wearing as protection. Let them experience freedom beyond their wildest dreams. In the name of Jesus, amen.

SECTION 1:
GOD WANTS YOU FREE

GOD'S WILL IS FREEDOM

I t was for freedom that Christ set us free; therefore keep standing firm and do not be subject again to a yoke of slavery. (Gal 5:1 NASB)

God wants you free. If you are seeking freedom, this truth needs to settle in your heart and mind. Everything that Jesus ministered when he was on earth was to bring freedom to people. He never failed to respond to someone's cry for help. Early in his public ministry, he entered the synagogue, opened a scroll, and read from Isaiah 61:

> The Spirit of the Lord is on me, because he has anointed me to preach good news to the poor. He has sent me to proclaim release to the captives and recovery of sight to the blind, to set free the oppressed, to proclaim the year of the Lord's favor. He then rolled up the scroll, gave it back to the attendant, and sat down. And the eyes of everyone in the synagogue were fixed on him. He began by saying to them, "Today as you listen, this Scripture has been fulfilled." (Luke 4:18-21)

In many ways, this passage is Jesus' mission statement. It is a reference to the year of Jubilee that occurred every fifty years. "During this year, economic debts were forgiven, land restored to families who sold to repay debt, and slaves sold to repay debt were to be liberated."[2] Everything in these verses points to freedom. Jesus came to bring freedom to the sick and the oppressed. He came to announce the favorable year of the Lord. Jesus' mission was to set people free.

---

[2] Bryan C. Babcock, "Year of Jubilee," ed. John D. Barry et al., *The Lexham Bible Dictionary* (Bellingham, WA: Lexham Press, 2016).

Many of us are not fully enjoying what God has promised. It is, in some ways, easier to water down his promises and, in this way, close the gap between what he promised and where people are living. When faced with difficulties, it can seem easy to settle for less than what God promised. The Bible declares that we should "not be anxious about anything" (Phil 4:6a NIV). Despite that promise, I have heard preachers say that we can't live without worry; that Jesus will give us tools to manage our anxiety. Thinking like that weakens the promise of God and deprives it of its ability to transform. All the promises of God are "yes and amen" (2 Cor 1:20). God's promises are a revelation of his will for his children. The promises of God reveal what is possible — what God's will is for each of us. Whether we ever experience it or not doesn't change God's will. Let's allow the Bible, God's Holy Word to define what is possible in our lives.

It is not unusual that when someone suffers for a long time without any change, they tend to lower expectations. Please don't do that. Instead of bringing the truth down to match the level of our circumstances, it is far better to allow God's Word to lift us out of our bondage. Lowering the standard, as revealed in the Bible, to match our experience deprives it of its power to transform. Paul Manwaring said, "We are giving the world an explanation, but they are starving for a demonstration."[3] A god who doesn't bring freedom is not the God of Abraham, Isaac, and Jacob. That is not the God of the Bible. Study the scriptures, and you will see that God desires you to be free.[4]

---

[3] Quote from sermon given at Bethel Church, Redding, CA.

[4] I don't believe in lowering the standard as revealed in the Bible to match our experience. However, neither do I believe in beating people up or blaming them when the healing we are praying for doesn't happen. To do so would be to act like Job's comforters. I am in no way asserting that our failure to receive is necessarily a result of our lack of faith, sin in our lives or anything else. Sometimes we just don't know why something didn't happen and we have to leave it like that.

A god who doesn't bring freedom
is not the God of Abraham, Isaac, and Jacob.
That is not the God of the Bible.

Not only does God want you free, but he is also committed to your freedom. Scripture states that Jesus came to set us free. "It was for freedom that Christ set us free" (Gal 5:1). God is invested in your freedom. Freedom is not just some strange nebulous concept. Jesus set us free so that we could be free. God is a good father. And as a good father, he desires what is best for his children.

A FATHER'S LOVE

I grew up with asthma. When I was five, my family moved from Brooklyn to a big old house on Long Island. My father loved that house. But he soon became convinced that the big old house, with its plaster walls and big yard full of trees, was not good for my asthma. He decided that the best thing for me was to move back to Brooklyn. We almost bought an apartment in Brooklyn, but at the last minute, a train came by and shook the whole building. That killed the deal. Ultimately, my father did more research, and we moved to a newer house on Long Island.

What does that have to do with the love of God? I didn't know until many years later that my father hated Brooklyn. He grew up poor. He had to go to work when he was sixteen to support the family. He had a college scholarship but had to turn it down. My dad eventually started his own business and was very successful. Brooklyn represented poverty to him. I later found out that he would wake up in the middle of the night in a cold sweat with nightmares that he was poor and living back in Brooklyn. As much as my father despised moving back to Brooklyn, he was willing to make that move because he thought it would help me deal with my asthma. It wouldn't cure my asthma. At best, it would moderate its effects. But he was still willing to move back to Brooklyn, the borough he worked so hard to leave, just to help me feel better.

We can all agree that my dad was a good father, ready to sacrifice for his children's well-being. My father's goodness, however, pales compared to our heavenly Father's. Jesus said,

> Who among you, if his son asks him for bread, will give him a stone? Or if he asks for a fish, will give him a snake? If you then, who are evil, know how to give good gifts to

your children, how much more will your Father in heaven give good things to those who ask him. (Matt 7:9-11)

Jesus is not calling our parents evil. He is saying that our heavenly Father is so good that compared to him, our earthly parents are evil. Imagine the perfect set of parents. Then recognize that our heavenly Father is infinitely better, infinitely more loving than any earthly parents could ever be.

But if God is all-powerful, and he is that good and wants me free, then why am I not free? Part of the answer hinges on the second half of Galatians 5:1, which says, "therefore keep standing firm and do not be subject again to a yoke of slavery." Standing firm implies effort on our part. God wants us free, but we have a role to play. Freedom is not just going to fall on us. It will take some effort. We have to cooperate with his will to experience the freedom he has for us.

***We have to cooperate with his will
to experience the freedom he has for us.***

We can see this clearly in the travels of the children of Israel. In Numbers 13, God has Moses send out twelve spies, one from each tribe, to spy out the land. Moses instructs the men to come back and report on the land. His instructions are:

When Moses sent them to scout out the land of Canaan, he told them, "Go up this way to the Negev, then go up into the hill country. See what the land is like, and whether the people who live there are strong or weak, few or many. Is the land they live in good or bad? Are the cities they live in encampments or fortifications? Is the land fertile or unproductive? Are there trees in it or not? Be courageous.

Bring back some fruit from the land." It was the season for the first ripe grapes. (Num 13:17-20)

God doesn't ask them if they think they can conquer the land. He has already declared that he is giving it to them (Num 13:1). The men return, all agreeing that it is a good land. However, ten of the spies declare that they can't take the land because "they are stronger than we are" (Num 13:31), speaking of the current inhabitants. Two of the spies, Joshua and Caleb, differ. "Then Caleb quieted the people in the presence of Moses and said, 'Let's go up now and take possession of the land because we can certainly conquer it!'" (Num 13:30). This is an excellent example of the fight of faith.

Will we respond to what God said or succumb to the circumstances? On the one hand, the Israelites were facing what looked like insurmountable odds. On the other hand, they had the promise of God that he was giving them the land. Which one would they believe? Ultimately, the children of Israel accepted the negative report of the ten spies. As a result of their unbelief, all the men who were twenty years old and older died in the wilderness. Joshua and Caleb, however, believed God, and went into the promised land.

"Therefore, since the promise to enter his rest remains, let us beware that none of you be found to have fallen short" (Heb 4:1). God is talking about the children of Israel's failure to enter the promised land, how all the males who were twenty years old and older, except for Joshua and Caleb, died in the wilderness. Their failure did not nullify God's promise. God's promise remains. It is eternal. It is never revoked (Rom 11:29). Whether or not anyone ever receives the benefits of the promise does not change it. We may never enter into all God has for us, but that shouldn't keep us from moving forward toward what he has promised.

It is essential to understand that these stories are in the Bible as examples for us, that they were "written for our instruction" (1 Cor 10:11). Freedom is God's will, but it is not automatic. It is up to us to choose (Deut 30:19).

So how do you live free? You don't directly choose freedom. There is no switch marked freedom that you can flip and instantly be free. You choose freedom by choosing to walk with God and his ways. It's similar to deciding to lose weight. You don't wake up one morning and say, "I want to be thin," and automatically lose 20 pounds (although that would be nice). You choose a healthy lifestyle. You eat the right foods in the right amount. You exercise regularly (all of this sounds remarkably depressing, but I digress). And the result of those choices is weight loss. In the same way, when we walk in God's ways, the result is freedom.

There is no flowchart or set of formulaic steps to freedom. Freedom is found in the person of Jesus. As we learn to follow him, he sets us free. Freedom comes to different people in different ways. In some instances, it can be dramatic, seemingly instantaneous. At other times it can be gradual. Sometimes it may feel effortless, while at other times, it can be a battle. We serve an infinite God who has an endless number of ways of ministering to us. He knows what is best.

There is no flowchart or set of formulaic steps to freedom. Freedom is found in the person of Jesus.

Paul Manwaring was at Bethel Church when he was diagnosed with prostate cancer. Bethel has many testimonies of people being supernaturally healed of cancer. However, in Paul's case, it didn't come supernaturally. He went the medical route. Today he remains free from prostate cancer. He said he had to overcome the thought that he received a second-class healing.[5] Regarding freedom, our responsibility is to trust God and follow him wherever he leads. He takes responsibility for the rest, for bringing freedom into our lives.

I'm often struck by people's prayers, where they tell God how to answer their prayers. I remember someone praying for a Covid cure, and they said, "God, let it come from Israel." I appreciate the desire to bless the nation of Israel but let's allow God to decide how to do it. It seems that God rarely does things the same way twice. In 2 Kings 5, Naaman is told that his leprosy will be healed by dipping in the Jordan river seven times. In Mark, Jesus reaches out his hand, touches the leper, and the leper is cleansed. God is faithful to do what he promised but will not be reduced to a formula.

Dr. Randy Clark gives five principles to receive healing in his book, *The Thrill of Victory — The Agony of Defeat*. But he cautions the reader, saying, "If you turn these principles into laws, they will backfire. Actually, the devil takes the law and beats you up with it, if you turn a biblical principle into a law."[6]

This should serve as encouragement if you have tried to achieve freedom and have failed. The fact that it didn't come a certain way is no indication that God does not want you free. It in no way signifies that it is not going to happen for you. It should drive you to seek him, to take the time to hear what the Holy Spirit is speaking to your heart. He will always lead you into greater freedom. "Now the Lord is the Spirit, and where the Spirit of the Lord is, there is freedom" (2 Cor 3:17).

---

[5] Manwaring, Paul. *Kisses From a Good God: A Journey Through Cancer* (Shippensburg, PA: Destiny Image Publishers), 96.
[6] Randy Clark, *The Thrill of Victory — The Agony of Defeat*, (Mechanicsburg, PA: Apostolic Network of Global Awakening, 2011), chap. 1, Kindle.

In 1 Kings 17, the prophet Elijah announces a famine. God tells Elijah to go to the Wadi Cherith. He provides further instruction saying, "You are to drink from the wadi. I have commanded the ravens to provide for you there" (1 Kings 17:4). Eventually, the wadi dries up. God tells Elijah to go to Zarephath, for he has commanded a widow to provide for him there. Methods are temporary, they may change, but the God who brings freedom is eternal. If we rely on methods, we may get some results, but ultimately, we will be disappointed. We will never be disappointed if we rely on God and his faithfulness, for he is always faithful.

Relying on methods makes God smaller. It results in us limiting God. In our minds, we have decided how God is to do it, and as a result, we believe that is the only way the help can come. Being method-focused transfers trust from God to a method. Over the years, I've seen increasing numbers of people pray that God would give the doctors wisdom, that they would find an answer to their malady. Doing that limits God to what medical science can do. Then if medical science can't find a cure, the assumption is that the situation is hopeless. Instead of relying on a method, trust God to do what he promised in the way he chooses. He's been at this a long time. He has a solution before we ask.

FREEDOM IS GOD'S IDEA

It is helpful to understand that freedom is God's idea. Freedom is not something someone pursues in their own strength, relying solely on their ability. Lasting freedom is the result of walking with him, of learning to walk in truth.

"Then Jesus said to the Jews who had believed him, 'If you continue in my word, you really are my disciples. You will know the truth, and the truth will set you free'" (John 8:31, 32). Freedom is the nature of the kingdom of God. Genesis reveals that before the fall of man, there was no sickness, lack, or shame. All the dysfunction that people experience in our world today is a result of the fall of man — specifically as a result of sin. "Through one man sin entered into the world, and death through sin, and so death spread to all men" (Rom 5:12).

> **Lasting freedom is the result of walking with him, of learning to walk in truth.**

All of the world's sin, sickness, and poverty today result from Adam and Eve's sin in the garden of Eden. The first chapter of Genesis reveals how God created the heavens and the earth. He placed mankind on earth and told him to "Be fruitful, multiply, fill the earth, and subdue it. Rule the fish of the sea, the birds of the sky, and every creature that crawls on the earth" (Gen 1:28). God placed two trees in the Garden: the tree of life and the tree of the knowledge of good and evil (Gen 2:9). He commanded man, "You are free to eat from any tree of the garden, but you must not eat from the tree of the knowledge of good and evil, for on the day you eat from it, you will certainly die" (Gen 2:16). That sounds pretty simple. You can eat from any tree you want. Just don't eat from the tree of the knowledge of good and evil. If you do that, you're dead.

Genesis 3 reveals what is commonly known as "the fall of man." There is a serpent in the garden of Eden who is cunning (Gen 3:1). He talks Eve into eating from the tree of the knowledge of good and evil (Gen 3:6). Eve then gives the fruit to Adam, and their eyes are opened. They now know they are naked (Gen 3:7). They sew fig leaves together to hide their nakedness. They hide from God (Gen 3:8). Not surprisingly, he finds them. Sin and death are now in the world, spreading to all people (Rom 5:12).

Sin is the root issue of all the evil, dysfunction, and sickness in the world today. It is a killer. Sin is not a term many of us frequently hear anymore; it is not a popular term. But it was sin that sent Jesus to the Cross to die for the sins of the world. Without sin, there would have been no need for a savior.

We can see God's heart fully displayed in the ministry of Jesus. Jesus never turned away anyone who came to him for healing and/or deliverance. Everyone who came to him to be healed was healed.

Occasionally I'll hear someone say, "But that was Jesus." Everything Jesus did was in concert with the will of the Father. In the gospel of John, Philip asks Jesus to show him the father. Jesus responds by saying,

> Have I been among you all this time, and you do not know me, Philip? The one who has seen me has seen the Father. How can you say, 'Show us the Father'? Don't you believe that I am in the Father and the Father is in me? The words I speak to you I do not speak on my own. The Father who lives in me does his works. (John 14:9)

He goes on in verse 12 to say,

Truly I tell you, the one who believes in me will also do the works that I do. And he will do even greater works than these, because I am going to the Father.

Not only was freedom part of Jesus' ministry, it is to continue to be part of the ministry of his body, the church.

I realize that none of us have experienced 100% healing when we pray for people. It is tempting to lower our expectations and bring our teaching and faith down to the level of our experience. We must never do that. Instead, we must allow the Word of God to elevate our experience. Dr. Randy Clark, who has led healing ministries across the globe for over three decades, tells the story of how this revelation first came to him.

Once I was in Florence, Kentucky, at the second largest Assembly of God Church in the state. I was reading from Matthew 10:2 and didn't like that part about raising the dead because it embarrassed me. In fact, I would lower my voice when I got to that part, but the Lord called me on it. The Lord said, "You are embarrassed by that aren't you?" I said, "Yes, I am. I'm embarrassed by that. God, I am still struggling with seeing the sick get healed let alone the dead get raised." I then heard one of the strongest rebukes I've ever heard from the Holy Spirit to me personally. This is what he said, and I can still quote it to this day: "Don't you dare lower my word to the level of your experience. Don't you be an experienced-based preacher. Do not create a theology that excuses your lack. Do not create a theology based on your experience of not seeing the dead raised or people healed. Preach my word and let people's experience rise to it." Whoa! So I taught for the first time publicly about how to raise the dead, based not upon my experience, but through the stories I knew from other people who had done it. In that meeting, a man heard those words, remembered them and used that prayer to bring his boy back to life when he was killed in an accident a few months later.[7]

When we reduce our preaching of the Word to our experience, we deprive it of its ability to transform.

Once we realize that freedom is God's idea, that it is his heart for the world, it changes our approach. We don't need to earn it. Our prayers stop being attempts to convince God to do something. Freedom is the result of coming into alignment with his heart and his ways. This is what causes us to receive what his will is for us.

WHAT DOES FREEDOM LOOK LIKE?

Mankind is spirit, soul, and body

To understand what freedom looks like and what it embodies, we must first understand mankind from a biblical framework. The Bible declares that man is a triune being: spirit, soul, and body (1 Thess 5:23). We are not three parts loosely connected. We are an integrated being. The body is the outer man, what some may call an "earth suit." Physical death occurs when a person's spirit leaves their body (James 2:26). When the body dies, it is placed into the ground. However, the spirit and soul live on.

The spirit and soul together comprise what is often called the inner man. It is "particularly the center of man's being."[8] The spirit is what is often called the heart of man. It is the part of you that gets re-born (made completely new) at salvation. The Bible declares,

---

[7] Clark, *The Thrill of Victory - The Agony of Defeat*, chap. 3, Kindle.
[8] J. Rodman Williams, *Renewal Theology: Systematic Theology from a Charismatic Perspective*, vol. 2 (Grand Rapids, MI: Zondervan Academic, 1996), 94.

"Therefore, if anyone is in Christ, he is a new creation; the old has passed away, and see, the new has come!" (2 Cor 5:17).

Our spirits are made new when we accept Jesus as Lord. The Holy Spirit comes to dwell within our spirits. We become the temple, the dwelling place of the Holy Spirit (1 Cor 6:19). Revelation comes to our spirits by the Holy Spirit that lives in us (Eph 1:17-19). The terms spirit and heart can be used interchangeably.[9]

What is the soul? The Bible doesn't offer a precise definition for the soul (or the heart or the inner man). That doesn't mean that we can't derive a reasonable understanding. J. Rodman Williams states that "the soul can be spoken of as the inner life of man through which the spirit expresses itself. The mind, feeling, and will are all aspects of the soul in action."[10] If we look at mankind and strip away the spirit and the body, we are left with the mind, will, emotions, and thinking faculties. It is, therefore reasonable to define the soul in this manner.[11]

It is helpful to think of the soul as the guy in the middle. The transformation of the soul is progressive. This is why the Bible declares that we are transformed by the renewing of our minds (Rom

---

[9] Williams, 94.

[10] Williams, 96.

[11] While it is reasonable (and I believe accurate) to define the soul in this manner, it is important to remember that word meanings change based on context (where and how they are used). This is not just true of *Koine* Greek (the original language of the New Testament), it is true of all languages, including English. The New International Version of the Bible translates the Greek word *logos* 48 different ways. Which of the 48 translations are correct? All of them are correct in their context. The English word "fair" can refer to weather (fair skies), a baseball term (fair ball), justice (that's not fair), a carnival (we are going to the fair), someone's health (they are in the hospital in fair condition), etc. All of these are proper uses of the word. What is improper is to take one meaning and apply it to all the uses of a word. The word "soul" can also refer to a person (Rev 20:4) and to the inner man (John 12:27). While the definition of soul as mind, will, emotions, thinking faculties is accurate, it should not be applied outside of its context.

12:2). The process of sanctification (being set apart for God) takes place primarily in the soul. 3 Jn 2 talks about having a "prosperous soul." Many years ago, I heard Jerry Savelle say that a prosperous soul was where "the mind is renewed, the will is conformed to his will (John 15:7), the emotions are under control and the thinking faculties are selective."

The Apostle Paul admonishes the church at Rome. "Do not be conformed to this age, but be transformed by the renewing of your mind, so that you may discern what is the good, pleasing, and perfect will of God" (Rom 12:2). It is possible to be born again, to have Jesus as Lord and still be conformed to this age. It is not enough to stop at being born again, at accepting Jesus as Lord. We must continue to follow him, to have our minds renewed to his Word for transformation to occur.

The soul is the guy in the middle. In some ways, the soul acts like a switch. The Bible declares,

> For to set the mind on the flesh is death, but to set the mind on the Spirit is life and peace. For the mind that is set on the flesh is hostile to God, for it does not submit to God's law; indeed, it cannot. (Rom 8:6-7 ESV)

We receive thoughts and impulses from the Spirit of God, and from our flesh. The unrenewed mind will side with our flesh, while the renewed mind will side with the Spirit of God. The Bible states that the flesh and the spirit are at odds with each other, and the solution is to walk by the Spirit (Gal 5:16). This requires having our minds renewed to kingdom truths.

> . . . in order that the righteous requirement of the law might be fulfilled in us, who walk not according to the flesh but according to the Spirit. For those who live according to the flesh set their minds on the things of the flesh, but those who live according to the Spirit set their minds on

the things of the Spirit. For to set the mind on the flesh is death, but to set the mind on the Spirit is life and peace. For the mind that is set on the flesh is hostile to God, for it does not submit to God's law; indeed, it cannot. Those who are in the flesh cannot please God. (Rom 8:4-8 ESV)

To please God, we must walk by the Spirit, not the flesh. And to do that, our minds must be set on the Spirit. Another way of saying this is that we must have a spiritual, not a fleshly, mindset. Romans 12:2 tells us that we are "transformed by the renewing of our minds." Renewing our minds changes our thinking. We begin to think in alignment with God and his ways. We must learn to walk with the one who sets us free to find lasting freedom.

SHALOM AND SOZO

Another way to understand freedom is through two important biblical words: *shalom* in the Old Testament and *sozo* in the New Testament.

Shalom

The word *shalom* is used 232 times in the Old Testament. The meaning behind *shalom* is "of completion and fulfillment-of entering into a state of wholeness and unity."[12]

Shalom is translated as peace 111 times. One example is in what is known as the Aaronic benediction. God says, "May the Lord look with favor on you and give you peace" (Num 6:26).

Sixteen times, it is translated as safe, with the idea of being secure, as in Job 21:9: "Their homes are safe and free from fear; the rod of God is not on them" (NIV). Other translations, such as the CSB, translate *shalom* in this passage as secure.

---

[12] G. Lloyd Carr, "2401 שָׁלֵם," ed. R. Laird Harris, Gleason L. Archer Jr., and Bruce K. Waltke, *Theological Wordbook of the Old Testament* (Chicago: Moody Press, 1999), 930.

The word is translated as prosper seven times as in Jer 29:11 (NIV), where God says he has "plans to prosper you."

Twice it is translated as a blessing as in Jer 16:5 (NIV), where it says, "Go back to the city with my blessing."

Five times the New American Standard translates *shalom* as well-being as in Isa 53:5, which reads, "the chastening for our well-being fell upon him." Isaiah 53 is a messianic chapter revealing God's redemptive plan, which was fulfilled at the cross.

It is clear that the word *shalom* has a much weightier meaning than just feeling peaceful. Entering into a state of *shalom* is a place of security, safety, wholeness, and well-being.

Sozo

In the New Testament, we have the word *sozo*. Many of us are aware that *sozo* is the Greek word that means "saved." While that is true, the word has a far richer meaning than spiritual salvation. *Sozo* means to "save, keep from harm, preserve, rescue." It carries with it the idea of being rescued or delivered, including being delivered from illness.[13]

Sozo is used 54 times in the gospels. Fourteen relate to deliverance from disease or demon possession; twenty times, it refers to the rescue of physical life from some impending peril or instant death (healing); the remaining twenty times, the reference is to spiritual salvation. The majority of times *sozo* appears in the gospels, it refers to something other than spiritual salvation. This is not to minimize the importance of eternal salvation but to emphasize that salvation is both now, in this life, and after death.

---

[13] C. Brown and J. Schneider, "Σῴζω," ed. Lothar Coenen, Erich Beyreuther, and Hans Bietenhard, *New International Dictionary of New Testament Theology* (Grand Rapids, MI: Zondervan Publishing House, 1986), 205.

Examples where salvation refers to healing and safety in this life:

- Mark 5:34 – the woman with the issue of blood was healed (*sozo*). Here *sozo* is used for physical healing.

- James 5:14, 15 – the prayer of faith will restore (*sozo*) the sick. Again, *sozo* is used for physical healing.

- 2 Timothy 4:18 – bring safely (*sozo*). Here *sozo* is used to assure us that God will safely bring us into his heavenly kingdom.

- Matthew 14:30 – when Peter was sinking, he cried out, "Lord, save (*sozo*) me." Here *sozo* means to rescue.

- Acts 27:31 - Paul said to the centurion and the soldiers, "Unless these men stay in the ship, you cannot be saved (*sozo*)." In this instance, *sozo* is used for physical preservation.

Sozo encompasses wholeness in spirit, soul, and body. Salvation is not just what happens after we die. Salvation includes healing for our bodies and peace for our minds.

The similarity between *sozo* and *shalom* reveal that the heart of God for mankind has not changed. God's intention regarding wholeness for humanity is not a new idea in the New Testament but rather one that reaches back to the very beginning and into eternity.

HEALING IN THE ATONING SACRIFICE OF JESUS

He grew up before him like a young plant and like a root out of dry ground. He didn't have an impressive form or majesty that we should look at him, no appearance that we should desire him. He was despised and rejected by men, a man of suffering who knew what sickness was. He was like someone people turned away from; he was despised, and we didn't value him. Yet he himself bore our sicknesses, and he carried our pains; but we in turn regarded him stricken, struck down by God, and afflicted. But he was pierced because of our rebellion, crushed because of our iniquities; punishment for our peace was on him, and we are healed by his wounds. (Isa 53:2-5)

This passage is a messianic prophecy concerning Jesus' vicarious suffering (suffering in our place). Jesus' sacrifice on the cross covered the needs of the entire person. If you need healing, the cross covers it. If you need peace, the cross covers it. Whether the need is physical, emotional, or spiritual, the cross covers it.

There are two common misconceptions about this passage that need to be addressed. The first is the idea of spiritual healing. This is a misnomer. When someone accepts Jesus as Lord, they are not spiritually healed; they are born again. They were not just spiritually sick. They were dead. Ephesians 2:1 says that we were dead in our trespasses and sins. Ezekiel 36:26 says, "I will remove the heart of stone from your flesh and give you a heart of flesh." The human race needs a heart transplant, not just CPR. The new birth provides restoration of the fellowship that God desires to have with mankind. The result of the new birth should be someone walking in the fullness of our union with him, in holiness, humility, intimacy with God, and in the power of the Holy Spirit.

Whether the need is physical, emotional, or spiritual, the cross covers it.

The other misconception is that the phrase "by his wounds we are healed" does not refer to physical healing. This is incorrect. Matthew 8:16,17 states:

When evening came, they brought to him many who were demon-possessed. He drove out the spirits with a word and healed all who were sick, so that what was spoken through the prophet Isaiah might be fulfilled: He himself took our weaknesses and carried our diseases.

This Scripture clearly shows us that Isaiah 53:4, 5 refers to physical healing, revealing that physical healing is part of the atonement. Our freedom is already bought and paid for. Getting free is primarily a matter of accepting what Jesus has already provided.

Freedom, Wholeness Was Part of Jesus' Mission Statement

He came to Nazareth, where he had been brought up. As usual, he entered the synagogue on the Sabbath day and stood up to read. The scroll of the prophet Isaiah was given to him, and unrolling the scroll, he found the place where it was written: The Spirit of the Lord is on me, because he has anointed me to preach good news to the poor. *(Isa 61:1 adds, He has sent me to heal the brokenhearted).* He has sent me to proclaim release to the captives and recovery of sight to the blind, to set free the oppressed, to proclaim the year of the Lord's favor. He then rolled up the scroll, gave it back to the attendant, and sat down. And the eyes of everyone in the synagogue were fixed on him. He began by saying to them, "Today as you listen, this Scripture has been fulfilled." (Luke 4:16-20)

Jesus returns home and enters the synagogue on the Sabbath. This is his first public preaching back in his hometown. Synagogues later followed regular lectionary readings, but in this period, readers had more freedom to choose the reading from the Prophets.[14]

---

[14] Craig S. Keener, *The IVP Bible Background Commentary: New Testament* (Downers Grove, IL: InterVarsity Press, 1993), Lk 4:17.

In many ways, this is his mission statement - what he came to do. As we can see, his mission is about bringing freedom to the whole person - spirit, soul, and body. The "year of the Lord's favor" was a reference to the year of Jubilee, a year of freedom. During the year of Jubilee, all slaves were released, and all debts were forgiven. All land was returned to the original owner.

When Jesus is finished reading this portion of Scripture, he sits down and tells everyone that "this Scripture has been fulfilled" (Luke 4:20). Craig Keener notes that "People rightly expected this text to be fulfilled only in the Messianic era, the time of God's coming kingdom."[15]

Studying the life of Jesus reveals that his entire ministry brought freedom to those who were oppressed. Whether people were sick or bound by sin, Jesus came to set them free. There is not one instance where someone came to Jesus looking for freedom and left without receiving their healing, their deliverance.

Acts 10:38 says, "How God anointed Jesus of Nazareth with the Holy Spirit and with power, and how he went about doing good and healing all who were under the tyranny of the devil, because God was with him." Jesus' earthly ministry was a precursor for what he accomplished on the cross. While on earth, he brought freedom to the multitude. He paid the penalty for our sins on the cross so that all might experience freedom. This includes inner (emotional) healing.

---

[15] Craig S. Keener and John H. Walton, eds., *NIV Cultural Backgrounds Study Bible: Bringing to Life the Ancient World of Scripture* (Grand Rapids, MI: Zondervan, 2016), 1749.

Emotional Healing

Emotional or inner healing targets the soul.[16] It is designed to identify wounds and lies that hinder intimacy with the Godhead. As wounds and lies are exposed and replaced by truth, freedom, and intimacy with God result. People who experience trauma, sexual abuse, and rejection often need emotional healing. Rob Reimer writes, "It is often the issues of the soul that keep us from intimacy with God and others."[17]

Everyone experiences emotional wounding in their lives. Having a healthy soul (mind, will, emotions, thinking faculties) requires learning how to feed and guard our minds and hearts and receive healing from wounds. As people receive healing and walk in truth, their souls experience the peace, the joy that Jesus died to provide.

Qualities of an Emotionally Healthy Christian

What does an emotionally healthy Christian look like? The most straightforward answer is the fruit of the Spirit. "But the fruit of the Spirit is love, joy, peace, patience, kindness, goodness, faithfulness, gentleness, and self-control. The law is not against such things" (Gal 5:22).

Paul contrasts the fruit of the Spirit with the works of the flesh[18]. Notice that the flesh works, but the Spirit bears fruit. One can never hope to manifest the fruit of the Spirit solely through human effort. Our strivings will never bring the peace, the contentment

---

[16] The terms emotional healing and inner healing are used synonymously throughout this book.

[17] Reimer, Rob, *Soul Care: 7 Transformational Principles for a Healthy Soul,* (Franklin, TN: Carpenter's Son Publishing, 2016), Introduction, Kindle.

[18] The flesh in this sense denotes the whole personality of man as organized in the wrong direction, as directed to earthly pursuits rather than the service of God. L. L. Morris, "Flesh," ed. D. R. W. Wood et al., *New Bible Dictionary* (Leicester, England; Downers Grove, IL: InterVarsity Press, 1996), 371.

we desire. But as we follow his leading and obey him, his fruit is produced in our lives. The fruit results from a lifestyle of walking with him, following the leading of the Spirit as opposed to the dictates of the flesh (Gal 5:16).

This is in stark contrast to the ways of this world's system, which values achievement and is based on our own efforts. We are told to try harder. But the contentment, the peace we desire, is not from this world. It is the peace that Jesus provides (John 14:27). Only as we submit to him can we experience this peace.

One of the most prominent qualities of someone who is emotionally healthy is contentment.

I know how to make do with little, and I know how to make do with a lot. In any and all circumstances I have learned the secret of being content—whether well fed or hungry, whether in abundance or in need. I am able to do all things through him who strengthens me. (Phil 4:12-13)

People often quote v13, "I can do all things through him who strengthens me." However, if we look at this verse in context, it is clear that the apostle Paul is not talking about all things meaning anything as much as he is talking about contentment. Paul has learned the secret of being content regardless of circumstances. Contentment is not automatic. But it can be learned. We can all learn to be content.

The word contentment carries the idea of being satisfied and self-sufficient. This is not a self-sufficiency borne of independence but out of dependence on God, who is the self-sufficient one. "For Paul, contentment springs from complete readiness to accept whatever God gives (Phil 4:11). He makes no distinction between the necessary and the superfluous, but simply gives thanks for everything."[19] Contentment is a place of rest. It is a place where striving stops. "In repentance and rest you will be saved, in quietness and trust is your strength" (Isa 30:15 NASB).

This rest is a rest of faith. The rest that God offers is not resignation. Resignation is accepting something we don't want simply because we seemingly have no other option. On the other hand, rest ceases from our human efforts because we trust who God is and what he has promised.

> Therefore, a Sabbath rest remains for God's people. For the person who has entered his rest has rested from his own works, just as God did from his. Let us, then, make every effort to enter that rest, so that no one will fall into the same pattern of disobedience. (Heb 4:9-11)

Is it possible to have peace, to live in a state of contentment when everything around seems to be spinning out of control? Absolutely. Jesus tells us, "Peace I leave with you. My peace I give to you. I do not give to you as the world gives. Don't let your heart be troubled or fearful" (John 14:27).

Jesus is contrasting his peace with the peace of the world. The peace the world offers is transient and circumstantial. The peace of God is far greater than that. "And the peace of God, which surpasses all understanding, will guard your hearts and minds in Christ Jesus" (Phil 4:7). "The punishment for our peace was upon him" (Isa 53:5). Jesus took our punishment so that we may have peace. We don't have to earn his peace. It's a free gift.

---

[19] Siede, B. 1986. "Suffice, Satisfy." *In New International Dictionary of New Testament Theology*, edited by Lothar Coenen, Erich Beyreuther, and Hans Bietenhard, 3:728. Grand Rapids, MI: Zondervan Publishing House.

My Journey with Inner Healing

I was born in Brooklyn (Brooklyn Jewish Hospital). Being Jewish, it quickly becomes apparent that you are not like everyone else. When I was five, my family moved to Long Island. We lived in Massapequa, which had the nickname Matzoh-Pizza because so many of the residents were Jewish or Italian. It seemed that all of the Italians (and many others) I knew were Catholic, meaning they believed in Jesus. Being Jewish, we didn't. We never spoke about Jesus except when my friends would turn on me and tell me we, the Jews, killed Jesus. This was not an effective way to witness to a Jew. It was evident that I wasn't fully accepted because of my religion.

We all face rejection at some time in our lives. When you see yourself as someone who is not accepted, it colors how you view the world. You view everything through the lens of rejection. This only serves to further the conviction that you are not accepted, that there is something wrong with you. That leads to being needy, which brings on further rejection. In fairness, I had a sarcastic, combative personality that didn't help.

After high school, I went away to college at Georgia Tech. While there, I joined a Jewish fraternity. One of the things we did was make fun of Christians. We thought Christianity was ridiculous. In my junior year, I became friends with a girl named Terry. She was the first person I ever met who acted like she knew God. I liked her, but I thought the idea of knowing God personally was weird.

One night we were talking in her room when two girls showed up. They said they were from First Georgia Baptist. My response was, "Sounds like a bank." They then asked me what I thought of Jesus. I told them I was Jewish, assuming that would end the conversation. After all, it always did in the past. This time was different. They again asked me what I thought of Jesus. I told them I thought they were nuts. I wasn't trying to be harsh. As a Jew, Christianity made no sense. The Catholics prayed to Mary. The Protestants I knew (we lumped them all together - the Episcopalians, Methodists, Presbyterians, etc.) would laugh at the Catholics and tell them, "You pray to Mary, we go straight to Jesus." As Jews, our response was, "Why go to Jesus? We go straight to God."

Then there was the notion of the Trinity, which no one could explain. To a Jew, the Trinity means you have three gods. You can try to explain it all you want, but to us, it seemed that the Christians believed in three gods - the Father, the Son, and the Holy Spirit. Monotheism is at the heart of Judaism. No way we will accept the idea of three gods, no matter how you try to explain it.

One of the girls simply asked if I believed in God. I told her I did. Hebrew school (the training you go through to be Bar Mitzvah'ed)[20] taught me that God was real. He was big, scary, and not that knowable on a personal level, but I had no doubt he existed. Her response was, "Why don't you ask God if Jesus is real?" I thought about it. My first thought was that I didn't want to anger him with such a question. But then I concluded that he wouldn't mind. After all, wouldn't he want me to know the truth?

I went back to my room and quietly asked God if Jesus was real. I didn't get an answer. I asked him a few more times over the next several weeks. I wasn't on a pilgrimage to find the truth. I simply thought it would be good to know if Jesus really was the Messiah or not. To this day, I can't tell you how or when I came to know that Jesus was the Messiah. It was a slow, osmotic process.

---

[20] For information on Bar Mitzvah, please see: https://www.britannica.com/topic/Bar-Mitzvah.

That summer, I drove from Long Island to Pittsburgh to visit Terry.[21] One night we were up late talking. It was July 4, 1975, at 3 am. We were sitting on top of a picnic table at a park outside of Pittsburgh. I remember looking at her and saying, "I've been asking God, and I believe." No sooner were the words out of my mouth than I was instantly drunk (I hadn't been drinking), and I couldn't move. This had to be God. It never occurred to me that it was anything else.

Terry looked at me and said, "Geoff, I need to go to the bathroom." "I can't move," was my reply. A few minutes later, she once again said she needed to go. "Terry, I can't drive." Eventually, the feeling subsided, and I took her home.

I drove to the apartment where I was staying, and when I looked in the mirror, I was disappointed that I looked the same. I knew nothing about being a new creation in Christ (2 Cor 5:17) as I had never opened a New Testament, but I knew I was different. It was kind of spooky. I slept with a light on.

The whole experience was very surreal. I didn't take drugs in college. I was not at all philosophical. I was an engineering student, and I was highly analytical. But I couldn't deny that something significant had happened.

Later that day, we went to a Fourth of July picnic with all of Terry's relatives. It was fun but strange. They were all fanatical Christians. Growing up on Long Island, I had never encountered anyone like that. Now, I was surrounded by these happy, strange people. One relative of Terry's was just sitting in a lounge chair, and every few seconds, she would say, "Praise the Lord." Terry's cousin Steve was having a good time, and he would say things like, "I'm

---

[21] Back then I would read my horoscope in the newspaper for entertainment. It would typically provide vague guidance. This time, was different. It specifically warned me not to travel. Things of the occult are real and are to be avoided if you want to stay free.

on the winning side." I wasn't sure what to make of this. Still, they were very happy, happier than my relatives at any of our family gatherings.

That night they all gathered around me in the kitchen. After all, they had a brand-new believer on their hands. They told me all sorts of things about the Lord. One of the things they said was, "The Bible is true." I went home, bought a Living Bible, and started reading it. Some of it I understood, and some of it I didn't. I started practicing what I did understand, and it all seemed to work. I never heard of anyone doing this. I thought I had discovered something new (I was not lacking in confidence). It was exciting. God had become relational. The Bible was a living document, not some religious treatise.

Not everyone was thrilled with my newfound faith. Being Jewish, my relatives were not happy. My father seemed particularly perturbed. This surprised me as he was not raised in an observant household and had never studied at Hebrew school. Throughout history, the church was one of the major organizations that persecuted the Jewish people. The Nazis used Martin Luther's writings to justify their antisemitism. Converting to Christianity was looked at by some as a betrayal. If you were an Orthodox Jew (we weren't, but I add this to provide perspective) and became a Christian, the family would have a funeral for you. While I didn't encounter that, I was not surprised that my newfound faith was not greeted with open arms.

In the fall, I returned to Georgia Tech for my senior year. Not surprisingly, some of my fraternity brothers were not thrilled at my conversion. However, none of this really bothered me. I had found something real.

After college, I went to graduate school at Carnegie-Mellon. While there, I became friends with a student named Mary. Mary had a sister named Joanie, who came out in the spring to visit her. Joanie was a believer, and we sat up all night talking about the Lord. Eventually, we fell in love and were married. That was over forty years ago.

After graduate school, Joanie and I were married, and we moved to Tulsa, OK, where I started work. Joanie attended a local Bible college. We would go to parties with students from the school. Some students had the attitude that those who did not attend the school were second-class Christians, with nothing of value to offer. If I offered an opinion on a subject, they would sometimes walk away, not answer, or act as if I was not there. Being unprepared for this treatment contributed to an increased pain of rejection that resulted from these episodes. The more it happened, the more I would respond out of the hurt, which only made matters worse. The fact that I had other friends did not matter. The fact that everyone faces rejection also did not matter. The rejection was all I could see. I had faced antisemitism growing up and rejection from my family and some of my Jewish fraternity brothers for getting saved. I was no longer Jewish as far as they were concerned. Now I was not spiritual enough for some of the Bible school students. It was beginning to look as if I did not fit anywhere.

I started to see much of my life through a lens of rejection. I would see things as rejection even when it wasn't real. I became needy, which only made matters worse. People would affirm me and tell me what a blessing I was. If ten people affirmed me and one rejected me, the one was all I could focus on.

I realized that all the affirmations in the world from people who loved me weren't enough to heal me of the rejection. For years I had studied the Bible on the subject of identity, specifically who I was in Christ. I taught it and would quote the Scriptures about the subject, yet the pain of rejection remained.

Everything started to change when Joanie and I attended a week-long healing school taught by Dr. Randy Clark. The healing school was life-changing, although not in the way I would have expected. One of the speakers at the healing school taught inner healing. I went up after his session to speak to him. When we were done, he asked if there were any issues with my father. I told him no, sure there were no unresolved issues. He kept pressing, sure that there had to be father issues. I left that session angry, hating inner healing. It seemed that inner healing was about people looking to dig up something that was not there.

After dinner, during the evening session, while worshipping God, I had a vision. The vision was a Little League team. They were wearing navy blue shirts and pinstripe pants. They were in a circle jumping up and down. While I could not see myself, I knew I was in the middle. I also knew that God was the coach. I was wondering why they were jumping up and down. I initially thought they were jumping up and down because I had gotten the game-winning hit. Then I realized they were jumping up and down because they were glad I was on the team. As soon as I realized that, I started crying and could not stop.

The whole vision lasted a minute or two (the crying lasted a while), but in that short time, God began to set me free from years of feeling that I did not fit or belong. I had spent years struggling with that very thing. I prayed, asked for prayer, read books, confided in people, and did everything I knew to do short of professional help, and all I ever got was temporary relief that felt like a bandage on a bullet wound. This was different. For the first time in many years, I felt the weight of rejection lift off me. God did more in a few minutes than all of my years of struggling.

That experience taught me that the Holy Spirit could do in a matter of minutes what years of counseling might fail to accomplish. The realization came that he was the one who delighted in setting people free. Not surprisingly, I no longer hated inner healing. I now saw it in a different light. I understood that the key to inner healing was to help someone connect to the Holy Spirit. He would do the rest, touching those wounded areas, replacing lies with truth, and bringing healing. Inner healing was no longer about digging around in the past to find something wrong. It was about giving the Holy Spirit access to heal those places of pain we desperately try to conceal. The experience completely transformed my view of inner healing and the need to have God touch and heal the wounded areas of life.

I understood that the key to inner healing was to help someone connect to the Holy Spirit.

I would like to tell you that from that point on, I never struggled with rejection. I would like to tell you that, but it wasn't true. Over time, the glow from that experience wore off, and once again, I seemed to struggle with rejection. While it wasn't as severe as it had been, there was no denying it was back. While at seminary, a friend took me through his inner healing model. While I got some freedom, it wasn't the breakthrough I hoped for. I was angry, discouraged, and becoming hopeless.

I have learned that hopelessness is a lie. As long as God is on the throne, there is hope. He is the God of all hope. Things may look hopeless. You may not know the way out, but that doesn't mean there is no hope. The enemy uses hopelessness to get us to give up, to accept the status quo.

"Now may the God of hope fill you with all joy and peace as you believe so that you may overflow with hope by the power of the Holy Spirit" (Rom 15:13). God is a God of hope, and he wants us overflowing with hope. This is an important truth. As long as there is hope, we can persevere. It's when we buy into the lie of hopelessness that resignation sets in, and we give up. John David Lewis states that goal of war is to "break the enemy's will. When that happens, capitulation follows."[22] When someone's will to fight is removed, they will surrender. The devil is a defeated foe. The only way he can defeat you is to get you to quit. One way he does this is by convincing you that things are hopeless.

As long as God is on the throne, there is hope.

I knew there was hope. There had to be an answer to my dilemma. There was no doubt that the vision I had was from God. It brought comfort and healing. How was I to sustain it?

Knowing that there had to be an answer, I sought the Lord. He took me to 1 Timothy 1:18, which says, "Timothy, my son, I am giving you this instruction in keeping with the prophecies previously made about you, so that by recalling them you may fight the good fight."

Years ago, I heard Kris Vallotton[23] say that if you have received a prophetic word, you better hold onto it because you will need it. I realized that the vision God gave me was a weapon, similar to a prophetic word that I was to wield as the sword of the Spirit (Eph 6:17). Every time rejection reared its ugly head, I recalled the vision. I reminded myself and the devil that I was on God's team and was accepted. The more I focused on this, the more I boldly declared what God revealed to me in that vision, the more secure my freedom became.

---

[22] John David Lewis, *Nothing Less than Victory: Decisive Wars and the Lessons of History*, (Princeton, NJ: Princeton University Press, 2010), Introduction, Kindle.

[23] Quote from sermon given at Bethel Church, Redding, CA.

The sword of the Spirit is the Word of God (Eph 6:17). This applies to both the written Word and the Word that God speaks to your heart. God has given us a sword. We need to use it. As we use it our victory, our freedom is assured.

There are people in the body of Christ who do not believe in inner healing. Some will tell you that you got it all at salvation (we will address that fallacy). I've heard others say all you need to do is "take every thought captive" (2 Cor 10:5). I understand their perspective. For years I thought inner healing was Christian voodoo. There are some practices in some inner healing models that are questionable. But let's not throw the baby out with the bath water. The fact that there is counterfeit money doesn't stop me from spending the real.

While it is vitally important that we control our thought life, if you've been sexually abused starting when you were a child, simply taking every thought captive (2 Cor 10:5) is not going to cut it. I have had the pleasure of seeing God set these same people free from years of abuse, suffering, and trauma in one inner healing session. I've seen people overwhelmed by his grace as years of pain, guilt, and shame melted away in his presence. When I minister inner healing, I get a ringside seat watching God set someone free. There is nothing better than that.

***When I minister inner healing,
I get a ringside seat watching
God set someone free.***

Biblical Basis
for Inner Healing

I avoided inner healing for much of my Christian life, convinced it was nonsense. I knew who I was in Christ. I could teach it, quote the Scriptures. I understood those truths better than most of the people I knew. Yet despite that, there were areas of my life where I just couldn't get free. It wasn't until I understood inner healing from a biblical framework and embraced it that I became truly free.

You may be reading this because you are desperate. You may have been struggling with certain wounds and bondages and are willing to try anything. Others may already be involved in inner healing ministry, and you are looking for additional insight. Still, others may think this whole inner healing thing is crazy.

One of the arguments against inner healing is that certain inner healing practices are not explicitly found in Scripture. Are we only going to do the things we see modeled in Scripture? We would then be forced to eliminate practices such as altar calls, counseling sessions, and worship conferences, as none of these appear in Scripture. Not everything that Jesus did was recorded in the Bible (John 20:20, 21:35).

Jesus says, "Truly I tell you, the one who believes in me will also do the works that I do. And he will do even greater works than these, because I am going to the Father" (John 14:12). Doing greater works means that we as his body will do things not found in Scripture. As counterintuitive as it may seem, limiting ourselves to the methods explicitly revealed in Scripture is not only in conflict with church history, it is not supported biblically.

I have an engineering background. Engineering is applied science. What engineers do is find new ways of applying scientific principles to solve problems. That is an acceptable way of applying biblical truths. God is infinitely creative. It would therefore be impossible for all of his methods to be expressed in Scripture. What we do must be consistent with biblical truth. I don't see anywhere in Scripture where the apostle Paul (or anyone else) had everyone bow their heads at the end of a sermon and had those who wanted to accept Jesus as Savior raise their hands. Yet we do this in many churches, and no one questions it. There are two primary reasons for this. The first is because what they are doing is consistent with sound biblical teaching, even if we can't find it done precisely that way in Scripture. The second reason is more pragmatic. It works. If people come to know Jesus as Savior and Lord, we can safely conclude that the results are from God, not the devil.

This is the way I approach inner healing. It is clear from the Word of God that Jesus came to "heal the brokenhearted" (Isa 61:3). Therefore, as long as the methods applied are within the bounds (the guardrails) of Scripture, we are on safe ground. In Mark 5, Jesus calls the woman with the issue of blood "daughter." Clearly, there is something more going on here than just physical healing. Jesus is restoring her identity.

In Luke 19, Jesus encounters Zacchaeus, a tax collector. Tax collectors often extorted money. They were considered traitors by the Jewish people. Zacchaeus' encounter with Jesus changes him from an unscrupulous person to an honorable man. Like many people in the gospels, their encounter with Jesus was life-changing as it restored their identity.

There are things in the Bible that don't seem to make sense and are not explained. Jesus put mud on the blind man's eyes and told him to wash in the pool of Siloam (John 9:6,7). Why did he do that? The Bible doesn't say. It's the only time he did that. I'm sure there is a reason, even though I don't know what it is. Elisha threw wood into the water to make the axe head float (2 Kings 6:4-7). The Bible is full of things like this. At the end of the day, we have the Word, and we also have the Holy Spirit, the Spirit of truth (John 14:17), who will guide us into all truth (John 16:13). If we are going to walk in truth, we have to heed both the Word and the Spirit.

There are ministry practices we learn from others. Many of us have been taught that one of the ways that people receive words of knowledge is when they have pain in their body where they don't typically hurt. How do we know that is a word of knowledge? There is no Scripture to support that. In fact, the Scripture doesn't detail what a word of knowledge is, let alone how to know when you have one. Yet many of us have been taught this because it works. In the same way, we use tools in inner healing simply because they work.

In Matthew 12, Jesus casts a demon out of a man who is blind and mute. The man is healed. The Pharisees exclaim, "This man drives out demons only by Beelzebul, the ruler of the demons" (Matt 12:24). Jesus' response is that a house divided can't stand. In other words, satan would never cast out satan because that would be a divided house, and a kingdom with a divided house cannot stand. Jesus said that we would "know them by their fruit" (Matt 7:20). If people are being set free and this freedom results in greater love for God and greater intimacy with God, then the results are of God, not the devil.

I ask two questions whenever I see a manifestation I'm unsure of. What's the fruit, and who is getting the glory? If the fruit is freedom, the individual is more in love with Jesus, and God is getting the glory, then the results are of God and not the devil. It's perfectly acceptable to do something that works, provided it doesn't violate God's Word or his ways. That doesn't mean that everything that was done was correct. If we had to pray the perfect prayer for people to get free, then no one would ever find freedom. God looks at the heart. Sometimes our intent is good even if our words aren't precise. As Bill Johnson says, "God translates."

THE VALUE OF ENCOUNTERS WITH GOD

One way that God brings transformation to people is through divine encounters. Encounters with God are a common recurring theme in biblical literature. God speaks to Noah and has him build an ark, by which he saved his family and condemned the world (Genesis 6). He speaks to Abraham and tells him to sacrifice his son of promise (Genesis 22). Moses sees a burning bush that is not consumed (Exodus 3). When he turns aside to look, God speaks to him, and the history of the world is forever changed. The three Hebrew children surviving a fiery furnace dramatically impact not only their lives but also the life of Nebuchadnezzar (Daniel 3). In the Gospels, Peter lets down his nets in response to Jesus' command and is forever changed by the event (Luke 5). It is clear God knows how to get one's attention.

God does not get someone's attention just to show off, nor simply to prove that he is there. Encounters with God are often life-changing, affecting individuals at a deep and heartfelt place in their lives.

Encounters with God are often life-changing, affecting individuals at a deep and heartfelt place in their lives.

In this section, we will examine two stories, the story of Gideon (Judges 6-8) and the woman at the well (John 4). Both of these stories involve encounters with God. These two stories are very different. Gideon's story is full of supernatural encounters starting with the angel appearing to him. The story of the woman at the well is very different. Hers is a conversation with Jesus. However, both stories have profound life-changing effects on them and the people around them.

GIDEON

We can observe God's process in transforming identity in the life of Gideon. Gideon's story begins in Judges 6 with the children of Israel hiding out in caves and dens to escape the Midianites and Amalekites, who would come and raid their livestock and produce. The Midianites and Amalekites would "come up with their livestock and their tents, they would come in like locusts for number, both they and their camels were innumerable, and they came into the land to devastate it" (Judg 6:5).

This is a picture of total defeat, humiliation, and fear. Nowhere do we see the children of Israel fighting back. They have accepted their defeat. In the midst of this, they cry out to God. In response to their cry, God sends an unnamed prophet who tells them that God said not to fear the gods of the Amorites, but they did not obey him. Like many of the prophets, his central message was that the people needed to repent and turn back to the one true God. The oppression Israel endured resulted from their disobedience and not their God-ordained destiny.

This cycle of deliverance and apostasy repeats itself through much of Israel's history (Judg 2:16-19). In response to their cry, the angel of the Lord comes to Gideon, beating wheat in the wine press to hide it from the Midianites. Typically, wheat would be threshed in an open area. In hiding from the Midianites, Gideon demonstrates that he has accepted the same fate as the rest of his brethren.

The angel greets Gideon declaring, "The Lord is with you, O valiant warrior" (Judg 6:12). This is the beginning of God's transformation of Gideon into a man who will be used to deliver Israel. Gideon responds to the angel by asking, "If the Lord is with us, why then has all this happened to us?" (Judg 6:13). He has endured seven years of oppression meted out by the Midianites. Gideon cannot reconcile the significant events of his people's history, such as the exodus from Egypt and their entry into the promised land, with the suffering they were enduring at the hands of their enemy. His conclusion is that God has abandoned them. Gideon's statement reflects the bitterness of his heart. Gideon's suffering has kept him from recognizing the presence of God. The message from the angel is in direct conflict with everything Gideon has experienced.

Interestingly, the Lord's response through the angel did not address Gideon's questions. He is clearly shifting Gideon's focus from that of a victim to that of a warrior. Gideon is being given a message from God, and he understands the message in that manner.

Through a series of encounters with God, Gideon is changed from a fearful man into a warrior that will deliver Israel. God tells Gideon to destroy the altar of Baal and erect an altar to the Lord God in its place (v25-26). For Israel to overcome the Midianites, they must turn from worshipping Baal to worshipping God. Gideon takes ten men and obeys God. He does it at night, as he is afraid of his family and the men of his town (Judg 6:27). Gideon's fear of destroying the altar to Baal highlights that his transformation is a process, not a one-time event.

The Spirit of the Lord then clothes Gideon, who sends messengers to four tribes to assemble his army. Still unsure about his call, Gideon asks God for a sign to ensure him that God is delivering Israel by his hand. Twice he lays a fleece before God. First, he asks that the fleece be wet and the ground dry. He then does it again, asking the fleece to be dry and the ground wet. Both times God answers (Judg 6:36-40), reassuring Gideon that God is with him.

The following morning, Gideon assembles his troops and camps south of the Midianites. The Lord tells Gideon that he has too many people and that they would boast that they defeated Midian by their own hands. God instructs Gideon to have all those who are fearful leave, resulting in 22,000 out of 32,000 returning home. Despite reducing the number of men by over two-thirds, God says there are still too many. He then has Gideon take the remaining men to the water, separating the ones who drink water by lapping like a dog from those who kneel to drink. The 300 men who kneel to drink are kept, and the rest are sent home. Gideon's army, which was once 32,000, is now reduced to 300 men. Less than one percent of the original army remains (Judg 7:1-8).

This is a significant change in God's relationship with Gideon. Up to this part of Gideon's journey, God has been extremely patient, repeatedly giving Gideon signs of reassurance. The appearance of the angel and the two fleeces showcase God's kindness and patience with those who serve him. To then have Gideon trim his army from 32,000 to 300 seems like a stern test. Through an ongoing series of supernatural encounters, God has brought Gideon to the place where he can trust God to deliver the Israelites with only 300 men.

There have been times in all our lives when it seems that God is asking us to do something that appears so far beyond us that it is scary. The truth is that he has been training us, shaping us for that very moment. He is a good father who leads and trains us, often without our understanding of what he is doing, preparing us for what is ahead. When facing Goliath, a young David recognized this. He tells Saul that he has killed lions and bears in protecting the sheep (1 Sam 17:34-36). This gives him confidence that he can now kill Goliath.

The Lord then instructs Gideon to go to the Midianite's camp at night. If Gideon is still afraid, he is to take his servant Purah with him. There they will hear what the Midianites say, further encouraging Gideon. Gideon goes to the camp and hears one of the Midianites relating a dream. "Behold, I had a dream; a loaf of barley bread was tumbling into the camp of Midian, and it came to the tent and struck it so that it fell, and turned it upside down so that the tent lay flat" (Judg 8:13). His friend replies by saying, "This is nothing less than the sword of Gideon the son of Joash, a man of Israel; God has given Midian and all the camp into his hand" (v 14). Upon hearing this, Gideon worships God, returns to his camp, gathers his men, and defeats the Midianites.

After the defeat of the Midianites, Gideon declines a request to rule over his fellow Israelites, stating that "the Lord shall rule over you" (Judg 8:23). He does, however, continue to function as a judge over Israel. His tenure as a judge is far from perfect. At one point, Gideon has everyone provide an earring as a spoil. This is reminiscent of Aaron fashioning the golden calf from the earrings of the Israelites (Exod 32:2-4). Ultimately the ephod, like the golden calf in Exodus, becomes an object of worship and ensnares Gideon and his followers. Despite his failings, the children of Israel enjoyed forty years of peace during the rest of Gideon's life.

How should Gideon's life be remembered? What can be learned from his life? The ancient historian Josephus claimed, "that [Gideon] excelled in every virtue."[24] William Koopmans believes that Gideon's life, in many ways, was representative of the nation of Israel, contending that Gideon "made a verbal profession of faith in God that was soon mitigated by selfish, sinful distraction."[25] The truth lies somewhere between these two views.

---

[24] Flavius Josephus and William Whiston, *The Works of Josephus: Complete and Unabridged* (Peabody: Hendrickson, 1987).

[25] William T. Koopmans, "Guile and Grief in Gideon's Gold: A Sermon on Judges 8:27," *Calvin Theological Journal* 37, no. 1 (April 1, 2002): 102.

While Gideon's mistakes should not be ignored, they in no way detract from his transformation from a fearful man into a warrior who God used to deliver his people. The man who defeats the Midianites with an army of 300 men is clearly a very different man from the one hiding out, threshing wheat in the wine press. While Gideon remains flawed, it is clear that his encounters with God have changed him.

The focus of Gideon's life should not be primarily on Gideon but on the God who transformed him. In many ways, Gideon's life is a testimony to God's grace and his patience. Time and again, God is there to encourage Gideon, to help him overcome his fears. One could argue that God delivered Israel despite Gideon's weaknesses. In that case, Gideon's story gives hope that God uses imperfect men and women as vessels to display his power and majesty.

This story is an encouragement to all who follow Jesus. When the angel first approaches Gideon, it's clear he is not yet God's great man of faith and power. The good news is that he doesn't have to be. He just has to follow God. Gideon's story is about God's patience in working with us slowly and enduringly until we step into what God has for us. It is encouraging to know that God is more committed to fulfilling his call for us than we are.

Notice how strongly the fulfillment of Gideon's mission is tied to his identity. God is willing to take the time to rebuild Gideon's identity. He is just as patient with us. There have been times in my life when I wondered if I was ever going to get past something plaguing me. But God is merciful, patient, and compassionate.

The ultimate tribute to Gideon's life comes from Hebrews 11, the great faith chapter. There he is mentioned with other heroes of faith, such as Abraham, Sarah, Samson, and David. These men and women are testimonies to God's transforming power despite their imperfections. Despite his failings, Gideon has his place with other men and women of faith, an encouragement to all who continue to follow the Lord.

THE SAMARITAN WOMAN AT THE WELL

The story of the Samaritan woman at the well is in stark contrast to the story of Gideon. Gideon was transformed into a warrior who rescued a nation and became its judge. In contrast, the Samaritan woman at the well is not a story of someone destined for greatness on a national or international scale. God does not transform her into an apostle or world leader. There are no references to her in Scripture or historical records outside of her encounter with Jesus in John 4. It is a story of God, in his grace, reaching out and transforming someone whom society considered unimportant, someone deemed unworthy by the Jewish religious orthodoxy. It is a clear picture of a loving God reaching out to all, regardless of their standing in society or background.

Jesus is on his way from Judea to Galilee. The Bible declares, "He had to pass through Samaria" (John 4:4). His encounter with the woman appears to be a chance meeting, resulting from Jesus resting on his journey. It is, in fact, a divine encounter, one borne out of the heart of God to reach those that society deems unworthy.

Jesus, weary from his journey, sits by Jacob's well to rest. A Samaritan woman comes to draw water. Jesus initiates the conversation with the woman by asking her to give him something to drink (John 4:8). The woman is surprised Jesus is talking to her and responds by asking, "How is it that you, being a Jew, ask me for a drink since I am a Samaritan woman?" (v 9). Jesus does not respond to her question. He clearly does not want to get drawn into a discussion of acceptable social norms. Jesus has a far deeper purpose in this conversation. Instead, he responds by saying, "If you knew the gift of God, and who it is who says to you, 'Give Me a drink,' you would have asked him, and he would have given you living water" (John 4:10). This is a cryptic statement. First, Jesus asks the woman for a drink. Then he responds to her question by telling her that if she understood who she was talking to, she would ask him for a drink.

The woman's response demonstrates that Jesus has successfully piqued her curiosity. She wonders how he will get the water out of a deep well. She then mentions "our father Jacob" to Jesus. Her statement clearly shows that she is still thinking in terms of physical water. Jesus responds by saying that whoever drinks this living water will never drink again as this living water will become "a well of water springing up to eternal life" (John 4:14). By making a reference to eternal life, Jesus is revealing that he is speaking of something more than natural water. The woman responds by asking Jesus for the water so she will never thirst or have to come back to the well to draw water. Her statement regarding drawing water from the well shows that she still does not fully grasp what Jesus is offering, and how could she? She is, like many people, so fixed on the immediate needs of this life that she fails to comprehend the riches of the kingdom of God. None of this dissuades Jesus from his mission to "seek and to save that which was lost" (Luke 19:10).

Jesus then tells her to call her husband. On the surface, this seems like a strange request, a departure from the subject of living water. The woman responds by saying that she does not have a husband. Jesus knows this and tells her that she has had five husbands and the one she is presently with is not her husband. He has now revealed to her that he is more than an ordinary man. Jesus is not looking to condemn the woman. That is not his purpose. By disclosing details of her life that he would not know except by divine revelation, he reveals that he is more than a mere man. The woman responds by calling him a prophet, a logical conclusion based on Jesus' last comments. How else could a stranger know these facts about her life?

At this point, the Samaritan woman recognizes the significance of her encounter. When Jesus revealed that he knew of her marital status, she did not ask him how he knew. She realized this was a supernatural word he could not have known unless God was involved. The woman no longer wonders why a Jew would converse with a Samaritan woman. Throughout their conversation, Jesus leads the woman into a deeper understanding of who he is and her value.

The woman turns the conversation to worship, saying that her ancestors worshipped on this mountain, but the Jews say God should be worshipped in Jerusalem. What started as a request for water has become a conversation about worshipping God. Jesus responds by clearly distinguishing between the Samaritans' beliefs and the Jews. He says, "You worship what you do not know; we worship what we know, for salvation is from the Jews" (John 4:22). This appears to be a potentially divisive comment. However, knowing the woman's heart, that her hunger for God has been stirred, this comment intensifies her curiosity. He then reveals that "true worshipers worship in spirit and in truth" (John 4:24). She responds by saying that when the Messiah comes, he will reveal all things. Jesus responds, "I who speak to you am he" (John 4:26).

Jesus' response is a clear declaration as to who he is. This direct response is very different from many of his vague references to his nature in the gospels. He is often obscure in his conversations with the masses and the Pharisees. However, with the woman, he leaves no doubt and no room for misunderstanding. He is openly declaring that he is the Messiah. Gerald Borchert recognizes that this statement completes the discourse by noting, "The particular force of the statement here needs to be noted. *The conversation is finished!*"[26]

---

[26] Gerald L. Borchert, *John 1–11*, vol. 25A, The New American Commentary (Nashville: Broadman & Holman Publishers, 1996), 210.

Immediately after Jesus' messianic declaration, the disciples arrive, shifting the focus of the conversation. Though they are surprised Jesus is speaking to a woman, they do not comment. The woman has been profoundly impacted by her conversation with Jesus. She knows this is not just a random conversation with a weary stranger but an encounter with the Messiah.

Knowing the journey's length, the disciples urge Jesus to eat. He responds, "I have food to eat that you do not know about" (John 4:32). The disciples interpret this as physical food. Jesus clarifies the comment by stating, "My food is to do the will of him who sent me" (John 4:34), referring to the harvest. Jesus stopped to speak to one woman, and in doing so, he accomplished God's will. Heidi Baker, missionary to Mozambique, recognizes the worth of engaging with individuals in declaring, "Whether God sends you to a vast multitude or to twenty-five people, he has called you to be significant. He has called each of us to live in his presence and to stop for the one he puts in front of us each day."[27]

The woman returns with the Samaritans, curious to meet the man who told the woman "all the things that I have done" (John 4:39). They come to believe in Jesus after hearing him, testifying that they believe because of what they have heard, and no longer because of what she has said. At their request, Jesus stays with them two more days. Baker observes, "Jesus reached one woman, but the woman reached an entire village."[28]

What is compelling about this story is that this is not about someone famous or destined for greatness. The woman at the well is not mentioned again in Scripture. She had five husbands. Whether they divorced her or they died, she lived with a sense of rejection. Yet the God of the universe stooped down and chose her as his

---

[27] Heidi Baker, *Birthing the Miraculous* (Lake Mary, Florida: Charisma House, 2014), 23.

[28] This comment was made during a Sunday morning sermon given by Heidi Baker at Iris Global, Pemba, Mozambique, June 8, 2014.

own. Francis Taylor Gench points out that Jesus' encounter with the woman is his longest one-on-one conversation in Scripture.[29] This one seemingly insignificant woman is valuable to God and worthy of an encounter with Jesus. We are all equally precious to God. He does not come to people because of their potential significance or role in the kingdom of God. That would reduce us to being pawns in a cosmic chess match between good and evil. God comes to each of us because he loves us and desires us to know him and, through our intimacy with him, to be transformed.

We are all equally precious to God. He does not come to people because of their potential.

The Samaritan woman's encounter is also significant as it was in many ways different than other encounters in Scripture. Jacob had a dramatic encounter wrestling with an angel (Genesis 32). Moses had the burning bush (Exodus 3). Gideon's encounter began with an angelic visitation (Judges 6). On the road to Damascus, Paul is knocked to the ground, sees a light, hears a voice, and is struck blind (Acts 9). The woman's encounter was not nearly as dramatic. Her encounter began with what appeared to be a harmless conversation with a stranger stopping to rest. Kenneth Hagin has said, "Many people are looking for the spectacular and missing the supernatural that is right there all the time."[30] The Samaritan woman did not miss the supernatural. She recognized that this was a divine moment, and her life was forever changed.

We should never determine our value by how spectacular our encounter with God was. I love hearing the stories of dramatic

---

[29] Frances Taylor Gench, *Back to the Well: Women's Encounters with Jesus in the Gospels* (Louisville, KY: Westminster John Knox Press, 2004), 110.
[30] Kenneth E. Hagin, *How You Can Be Led by the Spirit of God*, Second Edition, Faith Library Publications (Tulsa, OK: K. Hagin Ministries, 1989), 34.

encounters with God and the supernatural. It is all too easy to wrongly conclude that those with the most spectacular encounters are somehow the most loved, the most important. The truth is far more straightforward yet more profound than that. God is always drawing us to himself, wooing us into a deep relationship with him. He uses whatever means are the most effective to draw us to his side.

BIBLICAL BASIS CONCLUSION

Dana Hawkins insightfully declares, "we may not have seen the Lord face to face, but our battles, our times of wrestling with man and with God have forever defined us and are creating our legacy here on earth."[31] Gideon was hiding from the Midianites when the angel appeared to him. The Samaritan woman had what appeared to be a chance encounter with a stranger resting on his journey. These experiences were each unique and deeply personal. These accounts teach "religion is about the experience of transforming power."[32] As was stated at the beginning of this chapter, God has a way of getting a person's attention; these examples illustrate that fact. The wrapper in which the divine experience comes is not as important as the work he does in the human heart. God comes to unique individuals in unique ways that transform their lives. As a person encounters God and hears his heart, their identity is changed, and they are made whole.

It is comforting to know that God is always working on behalf of his people. Jacob and Paul were taken by surprise. King David was called when he was out tending sheep (1 Samuel 16). Moses was on the backside of the desert when he saw the burning bush (Exodus 3). Gideon was beating wheat when the angel appeared to

---

[31] Dana Hawkins, *Wrestling with an Angel: Fighting for Faith in Times of Struggle* (Springhill, TN: DPI - Discipleship Publications International, 2012), 13.
[32] Luke Johnson, *Religious Experience in Earliest Christianity: A Missing Dimension in New Testament Studies* (Minneapolis, MN: Fortress, 1998), 2.

him. Jonah was running from God, yet God arrested him (Jonah 1). The woman went to the well to draw water and encountered the Savior of the world. The common denominator in all these events is God's active involvement in fulfilling his will in the lives of men and women, even when they are not actively pursuing him. Believers can take comfort in the fact that God is faithful to see their destinies fulfilled, whether it is a dramatic encounter or a still small voice.

A Historical Perspective

Inner healing is a ministry that addresses the healing of the soul (mind, will, emotions, and thinking faculties). It can involve healing painful memories, past hurts, and emotional wounds. Michael Scanlan, a priest involved in inner healing ministry, defines the inner person as "the intellectual, volitional and affective areas commonly referred to as mind, will and heart but including such other areas as related to emotions, psyche, soul, and spirit."[33] Through the ministry of inner healing, people can be set free from lies and wounds that have held them captive.

The latter part of the twentieth century has seen an emergence of new, formalized inner healing models. These models spawned the development of ministries dedicated to inner healing. While today's formal inner healing ministries are a relatively recent development, the healing of the inner person has existed throughout church history.

Historical Basis for Inner Healing

Inner healing within Christianity can be traced back to the first century. Philo records how remedies were applied that "healed the souls of those who came to them, by relieving them like physicians, of evil passions."[34] Origen, the third-century scholar, spoke about the power of the Word of God in healing the soul. Origen comments, "stronger than all the evils in the soul is the

---

[33] Michael Scanlan, *Inner Healing* (New York, NY: Paulist Press, 1974), 9.

[34] Eusebius of Caesaria, *The Church History of Eusebius*, in A Select Library of the Nicene and Post-Nicene Fathers of the Christian Church, Second Series: Eusebius: Church History, Life of Constantine the Great, and Oration in Praise of Constantine, ed. Philip Schaff and Henry Wace, trans. Arthur Cushman McGiffert, vol. 1 (New York, NY: Christian Literature Company, 1890), 117.

Word, and the healing power that dwells in him; and this healing he applies, according to the will of God, to every man."[35] Similarly, Basil the Great spoke about the power of the Book of Psalms to heal the soul. He stated the Bible was not only "a treasury of sound teaching" but also "it provided for every individual need. It heals the old hurts of souls and brings about recovery where the wound is fresh."[36]

Gregory of Nazianzus, Archbishop of Constantinople in the fourth century, recounts how his sister was healed in body and soul through the Eucharist. He states, "She went away at once perceiving that she was healed, with the lightness of health in body and soul and mind."[37] Eusebius, Bishop of Caesarea, praised Theodotus, bishop of Laodicea, in observing, "he excelled in the medical art for bodies, and in the healing art for souls."[38] Eusebius not only distinguishes healing of the soul from the healing of the body, but he also establishes that healing includes the restoration of the soul.

John Chrysostom was a monk who eventually became Archbishop of Constantinople in the year 398. Chrysostom understood the importance of inner healing. He believed those entrusted with the care of the church had a responsibility to "train it up to a state of healthiness."[39] Achieving this state of healthiness

---

[35] Origen, *Origen Against Celsus*, in The Ante-Nicene Fathers: Fathers of the Third Century: Tertullian, Part Fourth; Minucius Felix; Commodian; Origen, Parts First and Second, ed. Alexander Roberts, James Donaldson, and A. Cleveland Coxe, trans. Frederick Crombie, vol. 4 (Buffalo, NY: Christian Literature Company, 1885), 667.

[36] Blomfield Jackon, *Prolegomena: Sketch of the Life and Works of Saint Basil,"* in A Select Library of the Nicene and Post-Nicene Fathers of the Christian Church, Second Series: St. Basil: Letters and Select Works, ed. Philip Schaff and Henry Wace, vol. 8 (New York, NY: Christian Literature Company, 1895), 45.

[37] Darwell Stone, *A History of the Doctrine of the Holy Eucharist*, (London, UK: Longmans, Green, 1909), 107.

[38] Eusebius, *The Church History of Eusebius*, 1:320.

[39] John Chrysostom, *Treatise Concerning the Christian Priesthood,"* in A Select Library of the Nicene and Post-Nicene Fathers of the Christian Church, First

required those in ministry to be "versed in all healing proper for the soul."[40] He firmly believed God delighted in healing the inner person. Chrysostom was firmly convinced that inner healing, or healing of the soul, should not be a complicated process. He believed, "the healing of the soul is a thing that is easy to procure, and devoid of expense."[41]

Inner healing was also evident in many Christian mystics' lives. A mystic can be defined as someone who is "deeply aware of the powerful presence of the divine Spirit: someone who seeks, above all, the knowledge and love of God and who experiences to an extraordinary degree the profoundly personal encounter with the energy of divine life."[42] One notable mystic was Teresa of Avila. Teresa was a sixteenth-century Carmelite nun who practiced contemplative prayer, where one communed with God in silence. She established convents where "young women could pursue deep lives of deep prayer and devotion."[43] Teresa believed contemplative prayer was the doorway to a place of union with God where "the soul enters into peace" and "all faculties are stilled."[44]

In her book *Interior Castle*, Teresa describes the experience of "guiding souls toward spiritual perfection."[45] Teresa believed in the beauty of the soul, warning against thinking "of the soul as

---

Series: Saint Chrysostom: On the Priesthood, Ascetic Treatises, Select Homilies and Letters, Homilies on the Statues, ed. Philip Schaff, trans. W. R. W. Stephens, vol. 9 (New York, NY: Christian Literature Company, 1889), 64.

[40] Chrysostom, *Treatise*, 64.

[41] Chrysostom, *Treatise*, 397.

[42] Ursula King, *Christian Mystics: Their Lives and Legacies Throughout the Ages* (Mahwah, NJ: HiddenSpring, 2001), Introduction, Kindle.

[43] Mark Galli and Ted Olsen, "Introduction," in *131 Christians Everyone Should Know* (Nashville, TN: Broadman & Holman Publishers, 2000), 266.

[44] Saint Teresa of Avila, *The Way of Perfection by Saint Teresa of Avila* (a Christian Classic!) (Colorado Springs, CO: Ignacio Hills Press (TM) IgnacioHillsPress. com and e-Pulp Adventures (TM), 2009), chap. 31, Kindle.

[45] St. Teresa of Avila, *Interior Castle* (New York, NY: Start Publishing, 2013), Introduction, Kindle.

of something dark."[46] She states, "The soul of the righteous man is nothing but a paradise, in which, as God tells us, he takes his delight."[47] Teresa believed a place of contentment could be reached through contemplative prayer. In this place, not only would the Christian find delight in God, but God would also delight in his children. Getting quiet before God and hearing him speak is foundational to many inner healing practices.

> **Getting quiet before God**
> **and hearing him speak is foundational**
> **to many inner healing practices.**

Another mystic was Madame Jeanne Marie Guyon, a seventeenth-century French Quietest. The Quietists also believed in and practiced contemplative prayer. Madame Guyon comments, "it is my highest happiness to see the reign of Jesus Christ extending itself in the hearts of God's people."[48] Like many mystics, Guyon understood the importance of an intimate relationship with God in inner healing. She believed "external religion has too much usurped the place of the religion of the heart."[49] To Guyon, "the reign of Christ on earth is nothing more nor less than the subjection of the whole soul to himself."[50] She believed the place of quietness before God brought healing to the inner man. She wrote, "as the air rushes to a vacuum, so God fills the soul emptied of self."[51] George Fox, Founder of the Society of Friends (also known as the Quakers), was another well-known mystic. Fox understood inner healing to be the result of consecration. He believed, "as people

---

[46] St. Teresa of Avila, *Interior Castle,* Seventh Mansions, Kindle.

[47] St. Teresa of Avila, *Interior Castle,* First Mansions, Kindle.

[48] Jeanne Marie Bouvier de la Motte Guyon, *Letters of Madame Guyon* (n.p.: A Public Domain Book, 2012), Reign of Christ in the Heart, Kindle.

[49] Guyon, *Letters of Madame Guyon*, Reign of Christ in the Heart.

[50] Guyon, *Letters of Madame Guyon*, Reign of Christ in the Heart.

[51] Guyon, *Letters of Madame Guyon,* Reign of Christ in the Heart

come into subjection to the Spirit of God,"[52] they would come to know the hidden unity in the Eternal Being."[53]

Spending time in a state of inner quiet is a common thread of all mystic writings. The mystics understood that, as souls sat in silence before God, they would experience his healing and transforming presence. To the mystics, all other activity was secondary to time spent in the presence of God. "Be still and know that I am God" (Ps 46:10 NIV) was a significant part of the lifestyle of mystics. As they spent time in his presence, they came to know him, and through that experience, they were made whole.

Inner healing continued to be an important part of the church in the nineteenth century. One of the significant movements of this period was the Holiness or Higher Life movement. Hannah Whitall Smith was one of the leading figures of the Higher Life movement. Smith believed a life of trust in God was the key to inner healing. In her classic book, *The Christian's Secret of a Happy Life*, she writes about the higher Christian life, which is marked by "an entire surrender to the Lord, and a perfect trust in him, resulting in victory over sin and inward rest of soul."[54] Her belief that resting in God brought contentment to the soul was similar to that of the mystics.

The nineteenth century also saw the emergence of several individuals whose ministries were marked by signs and wonders. Among these were A.B. Simpson, Andrew Murray, and John G. Lake. They shared a belief that holiness was central to the life of faith. Simpson believed that "dwelling in the secret place of the Most High" (Ps 91:1) was "the secret of holiness, peace, power,

---

[52] George Fox, *The Life of George Fox (His Memoirs)* (Harrington, DE: Delmarva Publications, 2013), chap. 2, Kindle.

[53] Fox, *The Life of George Fox*, chap.2

[54] Hannah Whitall Smith, *The Christian's Secret of a Happy Life* (Grand Rapids, MI: Revell, 2012), 34.

victory, and every physical blessing."[55] He saw holiness as a gift, not something earned. Simpson stated, "Our holiness is as much his gift as our pardon."[56] Andrew Murray understood the close relationship "between sanctification, which is the health of the soul, and divine healing."[57] This relationship applied not just to sanctification and physical healing but inner healing as well. Murray wrote, "Sanctification reminds us that true salvation and health consist in being holy as God is holy."[58] Simpson, Murray, and Lake firmly believed that healing applies to the whole person.

JOHN G. LAKE HISTORICAL BACKGROUND

John Graham Lake was born in Ontario, Canada, on March 18, 1870. One of sixteen children, he moved with his family to Sault Sainte Marie, Michigan, while still a young boy.[59] When he was sixteen, Lake first heard the gospel preached at a Salvation Army meeting. Soon after that, he surrendered his life to the Lord. Speaking of his encounter, Lake would later write, "I made my surrender to him. The light of heaven broke into my soul, and I arose from mackgroundy knees a son of God, and I knew it."[60] This would be the first of many encounters that would mark his walk with God.

Lake believed the Christian life was a life of total consecration and dependence on God. He comments, "the real Christian is a

---

[55] A.B. Simpson, *A.B. Simpson's Commentaries on Christ in the Bible* (n.p.: First Rate Publishers, 2012), chap. 11, Kindle.

[56] A.B. Simpson, *A.B. Simpson's Commentaries on Christ in the Bible,* chap. 11, Kindle.

[57] Andrew Murray, *Divine Healing [illustrated] [annotated].* (n.p: Niche Edition, 2011), chap. 27.

[58] Murray, *Divine Healing,* chap. 27.

[59] Roberts Liardon, *God's Generals: John G. Lake* (New Kensington, PA: Whitaker House, 2000), Kindle.

[60] Liardon, *God's Generals:* John G. Lake.

separated man."[61] He believed that lack of consecration was why many other Christians experienced a weak form of Christianity. He later wrote, "I learned by the Word of God and experienced in my life the sanctifying power of God subduing the soul and cleansing the nature from sin."[62] He believed that holy living was possible and that it followed an experience of sanctification.

John G. Lake devoted much of his life to the ministry of healing. This intense desire to see people set free arose out of desperation to see his family healed. He recounts, "For thirty-two years, some member of our family was an invalid. During this long period, our home was never without the shadow of sickness."[63] During this time, eight family members died. Sometime later, Lake's wife, Jennie, was struck with tuberculosis. The disease worsened, and by 1898, she was essentially an invalid. The sickness that had plagued his family growing up had now fastened its grip on his wife. Lake's dying brother and one of his sisters had both been taken to John Alexander Dowie's healing home in Chicago, where they were miraculously healed. Lake was called home to see another sister who was near death. When he arrived home, his sister was without a pulse. Lake sent a telegram to Dowie, "My sister has apparently died, but my spirit will not let her go. I believe if you will pray, God will heal her."[64] Dowie's response was, "Hold on to God. I am praying. She will live."[65] Within an hour, she was healed.

Despite these miracles, Jennie's condition continued to worsen. Feeling hopeless, Lake threw his Bible against the fireplace mantle. It fell open to Acts 10:38, "God anointed Jesus of Nazareth with the Holy Ghost and with power: who went about doing good, and

---

[61] John G. Lake, *Living in God's Power* (New Kensington, PA: Whitaker House, 2012), chap. 3, Kindle.

[62] Wilford Reidt, *John G. Lake: A Man Without Compromise* (Tulsa, OK: Harrison House, 1989), 21.

[63] John G. Lake, *John G. Lake on Healing* (Lexington, KY: lulu.com, 2011), 29.

[64] Liardon, *God's Generals:* John G. Lake.

[65] Liardon, *God's Generals:* John G. Lake.

healing all that were oppressed of the devil; for God was with him." When Lake saw the words "oppressed by the devil," he realized that God was not the author of sickness. A new boldness and resolve entered his heart and mind to pray for Jennie to be healed. Lake gathered people to pray for Jennie at 9:30 in the morning. The power of God came on Jennie, and she was completely healed. The effect of this miracle on Lake and his family cannot be underestimated. He believed the church's attitude that the days of miracles were past "robbed mankind of its rightful inheritance through the blood of Jesus."[66]

Lake's experiences forever changed his view concerning the power of God and the Christian life. Christianity became, for Lake, a life marked by the power of God manifesting itself throughout a person's entire being. While physical healing was a significant focus of Lake's life, these events helped develop a theology of healing not only for the body but for the inner person as well. These experiences helped mold Lake's own theology, that the life and power of God should impact every aspect of an individual's life, whether physical, emotional, mental, or spiritual.

John G. Lake was a man who walked in signs and wonders. He strove to bring the fullness of God to every person.[67] Much is written about his miracle ministry. Lake understood that outward manifestations resulted from a deep, intimate walk with God. He often said that the secret of heaven's power was not "in the doing but in the being."[68]

JOHN G. LAKE REGARDING SANCTIFICATION AND INNER HEALING

While John G. Lake is primarily known for a ministry of healing and miracles, he did not believe that the healing power of

---

[66] Lake, *John G. Lake on Healing*, 232.
[67] Liardon, *God's Generals*: John G. Lake.
[68] Liardon, *God's Generals*: John G. Lake.

God was only for physical illness. Lake viewed humans as three-part beings (spirit, soul, and body) and lived with the conviction that God's will was for the restoration and healing of the whole man. He firmly believed, "Sanctification is calculated to apply to the needs of all our nature, first to the spirit, second to the soul, third to the body."[69] The result of sanctification was holiness. Lake believed that the "inflow of holy life into our body *must produce* holiness in the *body*, just as it does in the soul."[70] Lake did not see this as merely a theoretical truth but a vital reality. Fellowshipping with God and having encounters with God produced a permanent transformation. Like the mystics, Lake understood that time spent in the presence of God was the key to transformation and inner healing.

Lake lived with an understanding that it was God's will to live in the fullness of divine life. Total consecration resulted in a person becoming "the utter expression of Jesus Christ to mankind."[71] The Christian life consisted of more than just dying and going to heaven. The Christian was to radiate the life and nature of God. It was God's desire that sons and daughters of God would walk with God and manifest the nature of Jesus throughout their daily existence. Living in the power, the presence of God, was the normal state of Christianity. This life of power was the natural byproduct of the life of God within the believer. This place of union with God resulted from complete surrender to God. The Christian life was a life without compromise. Walking with God meant walking in all of God's ways.[72]

The life of John G. Lake was marked by miracles of healing and demonstrations of the Spirit of God. Yet despite that, he understood that the work of the Spirit of God in a man's heart and soul was

---

[69] Reidt, *John G. Lake: A Man Without Compromise*, 21.
[70] Reidt, *John G. Lake: A Man Without Compromise*, 21.
[71] Lake, *Living in God's Power*, chap. 21.
[72] Lake, *Living in God's Power*, chap, 3.

more important than outward manifestations. He would say that the most significant miracle at Pentecost was not "the outward demonstration of tongues."[73] Rather, it was the manifestation of the love of God in their hearts that caused them to be "moved by God into one family."[74]

Lake viewed inner healing as a byproduct of sanctification and consecration. Consecration was an ongoing work of the Spirit of God that was necessary to maintain the mind of Christ. A life of sustained consecration would help guard the Christian from sin. Healing (both inner and physical) resulted from complete consecration on the believer's part, resulting in a person becoming a "Christ-man."[75] "The surrender of the spirit to God is not all that he demands. God demands also the mind and the body."[76]

Like the mystics, Lake believed inner healing came from understanding a believer's identity in Christ. He stated, "The secret of Christianity is not in doing; the secret is in being. Real Christianity is in being a possessor of the nature of Jesus Christ."[77] He realized that living in this new nature came from a renewed mind. Lake would comment, "Salvation from natural thoughts and ways . . . can come only through the natural mind being transformed into the mind of Christ."[78]

Struggles with sin resulted from a lack of consecration. Lake observed, "the things which possess the heart, and which are unlike God fasten themselves because the inner being is not subject to the will of God."[79] He felt that the church "has not recognized the

---

[73] Lake, *Living in God's Power*, chap 21.

[74] Lake, *Living in God's Power*, chap 21.

[75] Lake, *Living in God's Power*, chap 3.

[76] Lake, *Living in God's Power*, chap 3.

[77] Lake, *Living in God's Power*, chap 3.

[78] Lake, *Living in God's Power*, chap 3.

[79] Lake, *John G. Lake on Healing*, chap 2.

salvation of the mind from the power of sin,"[80] and that is why many say that "there is no such thing as sanctification."[81]

Lake's relationship with God led him to embrace his identity as a child of God. He observed, "The victory of the Christ and the victory of a soul is in the knowledge of the relationship between your soul and the soul of Christ."[82] This understanding of identity is key to modern inner healing methods. For example, Dr. Neil Anderson, one of the foremost Christian practitioners in inner healing, has stated, "Your hope for growth, meaning and fulfillment as a Christian is based on understanding who you are — specifically your identity in Christ as a child of God."[83] Lake's self-image was firmly founded on who he was in Christ. Lake's boldness was in knowing that the God of the universe dwelt within him. He had the utmost confidence in the Spirit of God who lived in him. He lived with the conviction that the Spirit of God in the life of the believer "was to be as powerful as the Holy Ghost was in the Christ."[84]

Lake would often remind himself that the God of the universe dwelled within him. In the morning, he would get dressed and put on his suit. He would then look in the mirror and recite, "God lives in that man in that suit of clothes. And where that suit of clothes goes, God goes."[85] Lake lived his life fully for God, completely secure that God was always with him. That assurance caused him to go through life victorious over sin, sickness, and the devil. He

---

[80] Lake, *Living in God's Power*, chap 3.

[81] Lake, *Living in God's Power*, chap 3.

[82] Reidt, *John G. Lake: A Man Without Compromise*, 31.

[83] Neil Anderson, *Victory Over the Darkness: Realizing the Power of Your Identity in Christ*, 10th Anniversary Addition Edition ed. (Ventura, Calif.: Regal Books, 2011), p 9.

[84] Reidt, *John G. Lake: A Man Without Compromise*, 40.

[85] "Faith," *The Cry of the Heart*, accessed October 21, 2013, http://heart-cry.com/devotionals/faith/.

lived his life firmly convinced "the man with Christ in him — with the Holy Ghost — is greater than any other power in the world."[86]

MOVING FORWARD

Inner healing, or healing of the soul, has been a focal point of the church since the first century. The church fathers, the mystics, and proponents of the Higher Life Movement all understood the importance of healing the inner person. While the methods vary, the goal of bringing "healing to the brokenhearted" (Luke 4:18) has not changed.

The specific focus of this discussion has been the ministry of John G. Lake. The fruit of John G. Lake's ministry testifies to the effectiveness of his life and what he believed. In his lifetime, he was responsible for the planting of hundreds of churches in Africa. When he returned to America, he opened up healing rooms in Spokane, Washington, and saw thousands healed and saved. His writings continue to bless and inspire many to this day.

Clearly, sanctification and consecration are necessary for a healthy Christian life. Lake's deep fellowship with God led him to understand and live from his identity in Christ. This is a cornerstone of modern inner healing ministry. In the words of Dr. Neil Anderson, for healing to take place, "it is important to recognize faulty beliefs from the past, to renounce them as lies, and to reprogram and renew our minds with truth."[87]

Is Lake's lifestyle an adequate model for inner healing? Lake's view of healing was that the life of God in the believer was to produce healing in a person's spirit, soul, and body. This resulted from an ongoing lifestyle of yielding to God. Through this process, Lake entered into an intimacy with God where he understood

---

[86] Lake, *Living in God's Power*, chap 3.
[87] Anderson, *Who I Am in Christ* (Ventura, CA: Regal, 2001), 7.

and embraced his identity as a child of God. These elements of sanctification, consecration, and identity are at the core of many modern inner healing models. By his own admission, Lake carried an anointing from God "seldom manifested in modern life."[88] His encounters with God were unusually dramatic. While his devotion to God is something the church can aspire to, it cannot be considered typical.

Current inner healing models are designed to help people encounter the love of God and receive healing. People often carry wounds from years of abuse or other trauma. Modern inner healing ministry typically involves a facilitator helping the individual identify root issues with the help of the Holy Spirit. In my own experience, I have seen people set free from wounds they had carried for years, unable to identify the cause on their own. However, through inner healing, the individual is empowered to connect with the Holy Spirit, renouncing lies and embracing their identity, resulting in freedom.

None of this is to discredit the ministry of people like John G. Lake. Knowledge is progressive. Isaac Newton said, "If I have seen further, it is by standing on the shoulders of giants." In many ways, today's inner healing models provide a formalized approach to help people apply the same principles men and women of God have used throughout church history to find freedom. Modern inner healing ministries build on the work of those who have gone before us to bring freedom to many.

---

[88] John G. Lake, *The Collected Works of John G. Lake* (n.p.: Jawbone Digital, 2013), The Strong Man's Way to God, Kindle.

SECTION 2:
GETTING FREE

Understanding Wounds and Lies

We live in a fallen world. No one is exempt from pain and suffering. Jesus said this: "In the world you will have tribulation" (John 16:33). There is suffering resulting from bad decisions. However, even if we always act wisely (which is impossible), we still can't eliminate pain and suffering. I lost several friends to the Covid pandemic. People who live healthy lives get cancer or other terrible diseases. We are not exempt from the collateral damage of others' decisions. Thousands of innocent people died due to the terrorist attack on 9/11.

Not all wounding is as traumatic as what happened on 9/11. We don't only live in a fallen world; we live amongst wounded people. People around us sometimes lash out at others for no apparent reason. Hurt people hurt people. People who are hurt, wounded, angry, and scared react from that place of hurt. We all have overreacted simply because someone "hit a nerve."

While everyone will experience wounding, we do not all respond to wounding the same way. Many years ago, Joanie and I were living in Texas. I felt a need to be alone with the Lord for a day or two and pray. I was looking for a cheap place to go as money was tight. I found a motel but had a terrible inner witness (call it a sense or just an inner "yuck" - a technical term) in my spirit. However, I let my fear of money override what I knew I had in my spirit. As the room didn't have a phone (this was long before cell phones), I went to a payphone across the street to call my wife. While on the phone, I got mugged at gunpoint. I remember getting punched and having my money and watch stolen. I got back on the phone and said to Joanie, "I have to go. I just got mugged." I can't imagine what she was thinking. Joanie called our pastor. Our pastor's wife was taking a walk around the block when God spoke to her and said, "You better get home and pray. Someone's life is in danger." She got home and hit the floor praying when the phone rang with Joanie's call.

I wonder what would have happened if she hadn't responded. I believe God would have found someone else. I had a broken nose but was otherwise unharmed. The broken nose required surgery. I remember sitting at home, praying, telling the Lord, "I know I should trust you with this, but I need some help." I then heard the faintest whisper say, "Trust me." I wasn't even sure it was God, but I was grasping at straws, anxious to hear anything. I told him I would trust him. I then heard him say (this was more distinct), "I'll go get my knife."

I've asked many people over the years if they knew what that meant. Almost no one knows, but I instantly knew what it meant. The knife was a scalpel. God was going to do the surgery. I canceled the appointment with the surgeon.

A few days later, I was eating dinner, and Joanie got up and started staring at my face. I remember looking at her and saying, "What?" She looked at me and said, "Your nose is straight." I went and looked in the bathroom mirror. God had healed my nose. My mom came to visit three weeks from the date of the mugging. I never told her about the incident, and she couldn't tell that anything had happened.

While I had to battle the fear of being alone in public places, no long-term trauma was associated with the event. I wondered why, but the answer was simple. There was a wound, but there was no lie associated with the wound. I didn't believe the lie that God didn't protect me. He was clearly trying to protect me by warning

76

me to pick a different place to pray. Even after I didn't listen, he had someone pray, and he spared me. He then healed me. The actions of the two men who mugged me were not personal. I was simply in the wrong place at the wrong time. Without a lie, the wound was short-term.

In 2009, Joanie and I were living on Long Island. This day she was having lunch with a friend. When she was much later than expected, I called the friend, who said she had left quite a while before I called. I then received a call from Stonybrook University Hospital. They told me she was in the emergency room and had a car accident. I asked how she was, and they said, "We think she has a concussion." I drove to the hospital, trying to stay calm, reminding myself that a concussion was probably not a big deal. When I arrived, it was clear that this was much more than a concussion. Joanie was lying on a board with a brace around her neck. She was in obvious pain and kept repeating, "I'm so sorry, I'm so sorry." They moved her from the board onto a bed, and when they did, she screamed louder than I had ever heard her scream. They inserted a catheter. What flowed from the catheter was supposed to be yellow (urine) but instead was red, indicating internal bleeding. I kept trying to get someone's attention without success. Eventually, they took her for X-rays.

It turned out that my wife made an illegal left-hand turn and was T-boned by a 6500lb commercial van.[89] She had four pelvic fractures, a broken collarbone, and internal bleeding. Over the next several days, we would receive several doctors' reports indicating everything from knee trouble to a fractured spine.

Joanie was quick to ask me to forgive her. She asked God to forgive her. She then had to forgive herself, which was a bit of

---

[89] Normally I would not speak about my wife in a negative manner. However, in this case I have her permission to do so. She wants people to know that God is there to help us even when the problem is self-inflicted.

a struggle. From then on, she kept saying, "I'm getting better," convinced that she would be fine. The four pelvic fractures lined up perfectly, so there was no need for surgery or a cast. They healed on their own, as did the broken collarbone. The internal bleeding ceased, and the other diagnoses were false. Whether they were wrong diagnoses or God did miracles, I don't know. I know she was completely healed, and we praise God for that. It took eleven weeks of hospitalization and therapy, but Joanie was back at work, teaching where she stood all day. Today, many years later, there are no long-term effects of her accident.

Well-meaning people told me that she would very possibly be traumatized, and I would likely have to get used to the fact that she would never drive again. I remember the first time she drove after her accident. We were looking for a new car as her old car was totaled. She had fear for a few minutes, and then it was gone. Joanie knew this fear was not of God, and she knew how to stand against it. Why wasn't she traumatized? There were no lies associated with her accident. She knew that the accident was her fault. She knew that despite that, God was there taking care of her, sparing her life. She saw God's hand at work throughout the recovery process. Her accident has become another testimony of God's goodness to restore even in the face of our mistakes. God turned for good what the enemy meant for harm (Gen 50:20).

If you fall and break your arm, there is typically no lasting soul wound. The arm heals, and you move on. But if the broken arm results from parental or spousal abuse, the arm will heal, but a soul wound remains. When people mistreat us, their actions tell us that we have no value and don't matter. If the abuse happens repeatedly, whether from one source or several, we become convinced we aren't important. It's a lie, but one many of us have accepted at some point in our life, supported by the way people treat us. These actions by others are attacks on our identity and who we are.

For years I wondered how some people would experience a traumatic event but would quickly recover with little to no emotional scarring while others would be traumatized by something that seemed far less severe. It is easy to label people as weak, but that only further intensifies the problem. I am convinced that it is not just what you endure. It is the lie that speaks to you in the circumstance, even when no words are spoken. The antidote to this is the truth. The more established we are in the truth, the more resilient we will become.

I have ministered to people who were in orphanages. In many cases, they quickly concluded that they were worthless, of no value, even if no one had verbalized that. Their circumstances speak loudly. People abused by their parents while growing up soon develop the conviction that they have no value, are an inconvenience, and are worthless. As long as they labor under that mindset - the lie that they are not valuable, they will stay bound.

Not all wounds stick - those that become part of our identity or affect our relationship with God are the most damaging. It is not the experience that wounds. It is how the experience is processed. It is the lie that speaks to you even when no words are spoken — the lie that you are worthless, stupid, and of no value. When lies are believed, the wound festers and grows. While the physical damage may heal, the lies provide a breeding ground for the wound to continue. Rob Reimer says, "when you have past wounds that get infected in your soul, and someone bumps against them, you have a disproportional reaction. These are like infected splinters in the soul."[90]

Years ago, I had rotator cuff surgery. After the surgery, I spent several weeks with my arm in a large immobilizer harness. It not only protected my arm, but it also kept people away. No one had

---

[90] Reimer, Rob. *Soul Care*, Healing Wounds.

to ask me about it. They instinctively knew that I had an injured shoulder and that they needed to avoid contact.

On the contrary, soul wounds are not visible and, therefore, not recognized by others. Without realizing it, people may say something or act in a way that touches your soul wound. This is exacerbated by the fact that the wounded person may not even realize what is happening. Often, they don't even know that they have the wound. If they are aware of the wound, they fail to associate the other person's actions as accidentally hitting a wound they couldn't see. They process the incident as, "This person hurt me," further intensifying the wound.

Wounds are breeding grounds for lies to flourish. Conversely, when we believe a lie, it provides an opening for a wound to form. So how do we get free? Three things have to happen for a person to receive freedom:

1. Forgive any and everyone involved. This is the first step in the process. Forgiveness creates an atmosphere where healing can take place. However, forgiveness is not the end of the process. Reimer states, "In the healing process, we will need to forgive the person who has wounded us, but even after we have forgiven, the wound itself often still needs healing."[91]

2. Identify the lies associated with the bondage and replace them with the truth. Dr. Neil Anderson, one of the foremost experts on inner healing, states, "Freedom from spiritual conflicts and bondage is not a power encounter; it's a truth encounter."[92] While I believe that inner healing is both a power encounter and a truth encounter, the importance of truth in getting and staying free is enormous. You can't get free without truth. Identifying lies and replacing them with

---

[91] Reimer, Rob. *Soul Care*, Healing Wounds.
[92] Anderson, Neil T, *The Bondage Breaker*, p. 23.

the truth is not a separate step, as it happens throughout the inner healing process.

3. Identify areas where the enemy has been granted access through sin or ignorance. As a person walks through inner healing, they identify the access points, the open doors where we have given the enemy access and close them.

The process is not linear. I rarely go through step one, step two, and step three in order when helping someone find freedom. Often this is a circuitous route, where we will jump around as the Holy Spirit leads. Sometimes forgiveness leads to identifying lies. Other times finding access points may identify the need to forgive someone. Identifying lies may lead us to forgive the people involved.

While this may sound complicated, it isn't. The key to all of this is listening to the Holy Spirit. The Holy Spirit is the one who "leads us and guides us into all truth" (John 16:13). Jesus said that it is the "truth that sets us free" (John 8:32). As we follow the Holy Spirit's leading, we are led into increasing levels of freedom in our lives. He knows the root issues and how to get free from them.

Forgiveness

Forgiveness is a central theme of the Bible. It is not only of paramount importance in receiving healing from wounds; it is central to the nature of the kingdom of God and salvation. In the Old Testament, the covenant sacrifices were built around God forgiving sins. "Each year, the Day of Atonement sacrifices reminded people of their sins that needed to be forgiven."[93] The writer of Hebrews demonstrates that the annual sacrifices served as a reminder that the sin issue was not fully remedied:

> Since the law has only a shadow of the good things to come, and not the reality itself of those things, it can never perfect the worshipers by the same sacrifices they continually offer year after year. Otherwise, wouldn't they have stopped being offered, since the worshipers, purified once and for all, would no longer have any consciousness of sins? But in the sacrifices there is a reminder of sins year after year. For it is impossible for the blood of bulls and goats to take away sins. (Heb 10:1-4)

For sins to be removed, there would have to be a perfect sacrifice that would not have to be repeated. Jesus was that perfect sacrifice.

> But Christ has appeared as a high priest of the good things that have come. In the greater and more perfect tabernacle not made with hands (that is, not of this creation), he entered the most holy place once for all time, not by the blood of goats and calves, but by his own blood, having obtained eternal redemption. For if the blood of goats

---

[93] Keener, Walton, *NIV Cultural Backgrounds Study Bible*, 2153.

and bulls and the ashes of a young cow, sprinkling those who are defiled, sanctify for the purification of the flesh, how much more will the blood of Christ, who through the eternal Spirit offered himself without blemish to God, cleanse our consciences from dead works so that we can serve the living God. (Heb 9:11-14)

Jesus' sacrifice on the cross was the one perfect eternal sacrifice spoken about in Hebrews 9 and 10. Scripture declares that "without the shedding of blood there is no forgiveness" (Heb 9:22). It took the blood of a sinless man to pay the penalty for our sin. Jesus accomplished through his blood what the law could never do (Rom 8:3).

Jesus' blood ushered in the New Covenant (Luke 22:20). Under this New Covenant, when one accepts Jesus as Lord, their sins are forgiven and they are made clean (Col 1:14).

What happens when a believer sins under the New Covenant? Once again, God has made provision for their sins to be forgiven. The Bible states, "If we confess our sins, he is faithful and righteous to forgive us our sins and to cleanse us from all unrighteousness" (1 John 1:9). Sin is not to be ignored. Sin left unchecked will spread like cancer. The response to sin is to confess it, turn from it, and know that God is faithful to forgive.

Not only does God forgive us, but we are also to forgive others. Believers do not have the right to withhold forgiveness. Forgiveness demonstrates the trust that we depend on God to defend us; he then hears our prayers of dependence on him (Matt 6:14–15; cf. 1 Pet 3:7, 12). Craig Keener observes, "Scripture is explicit that failure to forgive someone who is sorry plays into the devil's hands" (2 Cor 2:10–11).[94]

---

[94] Craig S. Keener, *Spirit Hermeneutics: Reading Scripture in Light of Pentecost* (Grand Rapids, MI: William B. Eerdmans Publishing Company, 2016), 271.

FORGIVENESS MATTERS

Why is forgiveness so important? Because there is no freedom apart from forgiveness. The old adage "time heals all wounds" is simply not true. Unforgiveness produces bitterness, and bitterness always results in bondage. Forgiveness produces freedom that allows us to pursue the purposes of God.

Why is forgiveness so important?
Because there is no freedom
apart from forgiveness.

Genesis 37-50 tells the story of Joseph, one of Jacob's twelve sons. Jacob showed favoritism to Joseph, which caused his brothers to hate him, and sell him into slavery in Egypt. In Egypt, he served in the household of Potiphar, an officer of Pharoah. The Bible states, "The Lord was with Joseph, and he became a successful man, serving in the household of his Egyptian master" (Gen 39:2). While Joseph did nothing to warrant being sold into slavery, God is still with Joseph and continues to bless him.

While serving in Potiphar's house, Potiphar's wife tries to seduce Joseph. His response is a model of integrity. He does not respond based on what is expedient. He holds himself to a higher standard – what is right in the eyes of God.

> But he refused. "Look," he said to his master's wife, with me here my master does not concern himself with anything in his house, and he has put all that he owns under my authority. No one in this house is greater than I am. He has withheld nothing from me except you, because you are his wife. So how could I do this immense evil, and how could I sin against God? (Gen 39:8,9)

Despite his response, Pharoah's wife continues her advances toward Joseph. One day she grabs him by his garment. Joseph escapes, leaving his garment behind. Potiphar's wife then lies to Potiphar, claiming that Joseph tried to force himself on her. Potiphar responds by having Joseph sent to prison.

Once again, Joseph did nothing wrong. God continues to be with Joseph, and he has such favor with the prison warden that Joseph becomes responsible for everything that goes on in prison. The Bible tells us that just as with Potiphar, "the Lord made everything he did be successful" (Gen 39:23).

Sometime later, the baker and cupbearer of Pharoah are put in prison for offending Pharoah. While there, they each had a dream. Joseph interprets their dreams, telling the cupbearer that he will be restored to his position in three days. Upon hearing the positive interpretation of the dream, the baker shares his dream with Joseph. Joseph tells the baker that in three days, he will be hanged. Both dreams come to pass just as Joseph interpreted them.

Joseph asks the cupbearer to remember him and mention him to Pharoah when he is restored. The cupbearer forgets, leaving Joseph in prison. While it is clear that God is blessing Joseph wherever he is, he continues to suffer at the hands of others. Put yourself in Joseph's position. How would you react? The temptation to become bitter is enormous. Yet Joseph maintains his integrity.

Two years pass, and Pharoah has a dream. It is at this point that the cupbearer remembers Joseph. Pharoah calls for Joseph, who interprets the dream for him. He tells Pharoah that seven years of prosperity are coming, followed by seven years of famine. He instructs Pharoah on how to take care of Egypt during the famine. Pharoah, recognizing the wisdom of God on Joseph, makes him prime minister of Egypt. Joseph seemed like a forgotten man, but God never forgot where he was or what he was called to do.

The famine comes, just as Joseph tells Pharoah. Jacob sends his sons to Egypt to buy grain. Joseph recognizes his brothers, and ultimately it is Joseph's presence in Egypt that saves his family. Joseph could have taken vengeance on his brothers for selling him into slavery. He could have sent his brothers away empty-handed, and they would have starved. As prime minister, Joseph could have put them in prison or worse. But he responds out of his love for his family and shows mercy. Pharoah is told about this and tells Joseph to have his family move to Egypt. Pharoah gives them land in Goshen to settle.

Jacob eventually dies. Joseph's brothers are concerned that Joseph still harbors a grudge against them. They send a message to Joseph saying,

> So they sent this message to Joseph, "Before he died your father gave a command: 'Say this to Joseph: Please forgive your brothers' transgression and their sin—the suffering they caused you.' Therefore, please forgive the transgression of the servants of the God of your father." Joseph wept when their message came to him. His brothers also came to him, bowed down before him, and said, "We are your slaves!" (Gen 50:16-18)

Joseph responds by telling them,

> Don't be afraid. Am I in the place of God? You planned evil against me; God planned it for good to bring about the present result—the survival of many people. Therefore don't be afraid. I will take care of you and your children. And he comforted them and spoke kindly to them. (Gen 50:19)

If anyone ever had a justification for seeking retaliation, it was Joseph. Instead, he showed mercy to those who hurt him. Joseph's attitude toward his brothers is a beautiful example of what it means for someone to forgive those who have wronged them.

Parable of the Unforgiving Servant

In Matthew 18:21, Peter asks Jesus how many times he must forgive. Up to seven times? Jesus replies with up to seventy times seven. He then tells them a parable, "For this reason, the kingdom of heaven can be compared to a king who wanted to settle accounts with his servants" (Matt 18:23). In this parable, a servant comes to the king. He owes his master 10,000 talents. A talent is 6,000 denarii. Each denarius is considered a day's wage. This amounts to billions of dollars, an enormous sum of money, a larger debt than anyone could have amassed. Since the servant can't possibly pay this, the master orders that everything he has, including his wife and children, be sold to pay the debt. The servant pleads with his master, and his master responds by forgiving the debt.

The same servant then finds another servant who owes him a hundred denarii. The servant asks for more time to pay back the debt. But instead of being merciful, the first servant has him thrown into prison. The other servants hear about this and go to their master. When his master hears this, he is enraged. He responds by saying,

> Then, after he had summoned him, his master said to him, "You wicked servant! I forgave you all that debt because you begged me. Shouldn't you also have had mercy on your fellow servant, as I had mercy on you?" And because he was angry, his master handed him over to the jailers to be tortured until he could pay everything that was owed. (Matt 18:32-34)

Jesus ends the parable by saying,

So also, my heavenly Father will do to you unless every one of you forgives his brother or sister from your heart. (Matt 18:35)

The point of the parable is clear. The first servant's debt is analogous to our debt before God. There is no way we can pay back our debt. Yet our gracious heavenly Father responded by sending Jesus to pay the price for our sins and forgives the debt. If he forgave us such an enormous debt, who are we to withhold forgiveness? The first servant will never be able to pay his debt. By not forgiving his fellow servant, he forfeited the forgiveness offered to him. Verse 35 is sobering. It clearly explains that we must forgive others to experience God's forgiveness. If we want to walk in freedom, forgiveness is not optional. Unforgiveness is not something that we can ever consider. We must be quick to forgive.

The Effect of Unforgiveness

Rodney Hogue summarizes the debilitating effect of unforgiveness:

Unforgiveness stifles God's destiny for our lives. It clouds our motives. It pollutes our purpose. It tempts us to deviate from our course. When unforgiveness is present, we find ourselves weighed down and easily worn out. When we have a heart that is willing to forgive, then the weights that hinder us are gone. When we forgive, we live in freedom – freedom is a great place to dwell![95]

There is no freedom apart from forgiveness. The Bible tells us that if we want God to forgive us, we need to forgive others (Mark 11:25). Unforgiveness is like a cancer. It is often said that it is like taking poison, hoping the other person dies. Refusing to forgive

---

[95] Rodney Hogue, *Forgiveness*, (Hayward, CA: Rodney Hogue) chap. 4, Kindle.

perpetuates suffering. Unforgiveness leads to bitterness. It sucks the joy out of life. It is a hindrance to one's relationship with God.

What Forgiveness Is

The essence of forgiveness is acknowledging that a debt is owed to us, followed by a decision to release the offending party's indebtedness. Releasing a debt is not the same as denying that it happened. Denial makes believe that nothing happened. If nothing happened, then there is nothing to forgive. Without forgiveness, there is no freedom. Denying what someone did sounds noble, but it does not produce freedom. If you have been wronged, acknowledge it, forgive the offending party and receive freedom.

It is common for people to accept blame for what happened. Only take responsibility for your part in the altercation. In walking someone through forgiveness, I have had people pray prayers such as, "God, I forgive them for being a jerk." Don't feel bad about acknowledging what you endured. Forgiveness means releasing what you are owed and will not give your offenders what they deserve. Forgiveness isn't saying that you are not owed something. Forgiveness acknowledges the debt, but you are choosing to cancel it. This is the essence of forgiveness – releasing the other person's indebtedness to you. You might want revenge, but no matter how much the offender may suffer, it won't remove your pain. The only way to be emotionally free from what they did is to let go and turn the offender over to Jesus. Forgiveness is not about you getting justice. It is about releasing the offending party so you can be free.

What is the proper response to being mistreated? We reap what we sow (Gal 6:7). If we allow ourselves to become bitter, we will sow out of that bitterness and reap more bitterness. If we forgive and show mercy, we will reap mercy. You determine your harvest. Which one would you rather have?

Forgiveness is not reconciliation

Forgiveness is not pretending that the offense never happened. Forgiveness is not reconciliation. While reconciliation is noble, it is not always possible or wise. Someone who has suffered physical abuse from a spouse does not have to let them back in their life. While forgiveness is a gift, trust has to be earned. If you come over my house and steal from me, I will forgive you, but I may not let you back in my house. One's forgiveness does not always result in the other party's repentance. They may still be dishonest, abusive. There are times when reconciliation is not possible. If they are unwilling to change their ways, then it may be necessary to love them from a distance.

In his book, *Keep Your Love On*, Danny Silk talks about relationships in terms of concentric circles.[96] The innermost circle is you and God. The next circle is you and your spouse. The third innermost circle would be family members or close friends. If someone wrongs you, you should forgive them, but trust has been broken. In this case, you may have to move them to an outer circle until trust is re-established. In some cases, they may need to remain there.

I was betrayed by people who I considered dear friends, who were in one of the inner circles. While I forgave them, reconciliation never took place. I continue to hope that one day it will happen. However, they are now in an outer circle and will stay there until trust is rebuilt. This is not in any way a vengeful act. It is simply using wisdom. God does not hold us accountable for the response of others when we forgive them.

How do we respond when people are offended by us? If we have wronged them, then we should apologize. Often I will apologize, even if I'm not sure I did anything wrong, simply to keep peace. I

---

[96] Danny Silk, *Keep Your Love On*, (Red Arrow Media, 2013) chap. 8, Kindle.

was walking into church one Sunday. I was preaching that day, and I was so focused I didn't even notice all of the people around me. The following week, a friend of mine came up to me and told me that I had offended someone by walking right by them. I had never even met this person. But my response was, "What would you like me to do? Do you think I should apologize?" In this case, my friend told me to hug him when I saw him. The following Sunday, I made a point of going up to him and giving him a big hug. Even though I don't believe I did anything wrong, it is often better to take the high road to keep peace when possible.

While it is essential to be quick to forgive and apologize when necessary, we are under no obligation to be someone's whipping boy. Many years ago, I was teaching classes at an evening Bible school. There was a woman to whom I spent a lot of time ministering. One day she got up in front of the church and told everyone I was a genius. However, several weeks later, she felt I interrupted her in class. At the time, I didn't realize it. The following Sunday, her husband approached me. He was angry with me and told me that I was short with his wife and threatened me by saying it wasn't going to happen again. I told him that if I wronged his wife, I would apologize. (I did apologize to her, but it didn't help.) I was more than willing to meet with them and reconcile our differences. He had no interest in that. He simply wanted me to feel his anger. Ultimately, I told him, "If you want to work through this, I would be more than willing to meet with you and your wife. However, if you want a pound of flesh, go somewhere else." Jesus never sought forgiveness from the Pharisees for offending them.

Forgiveness is always possible. God's grace is always sufficient and enables us to forgive. That doesn't mean it's always easy. There are times when we don't want to forgive. People sometimes think that the offending party doesn't deserve forgiveness. The truth is, none of us deserve the forgiveness God offers. None of us are worthy of his grace, his love, yet God extends his love to all time and time again. It is not for us to judge.

A common mindset is that forgiving an offender somehow relieves them of any consequences of their actions. That's simply not true. While forgiveness results in us removing any debt owed, it doesn't exempt the offending party from God's justice or possible legal consequences. Suppose someone steals from you, and they are caught. In that case, your forgiveness doesn't stop the criminal justice system from prosecuting the individual. Sowing and reaping continue to work in the lives of all involved. Failure to forgive hurts you, not them. Conversely, your forgiveness frees you but does not eliminate any consequences the offending party is due.

It is not unusual for someone to feel that they can't forgive. Forgiveness is an act of the will, not a feeling. A person may not feel like forgiving, but God never asks someone to do anything he doesn't enable them to do. Years ago, I was struggling with forgiving someone. The Lord led me to bless them as an act of forgiveness and mercy. I remember thinking, "I'm praying for God to bless them, but I hope he doesn't answer this. I'm going to be ticked off if he blesses them." Surely, this is not the most Christlike attitude to have. But as I continued to bless them, my feelings and attitude toward this person changed so that I truly desired for them to be blessed.

**Forgiveness is an act of the will,
not a feeling.**

I have ministered to people who have endured horrific acts against them. People who were sexually abused, who were raped, who had family members killed. In all cases, the grace of God was there to forgive, and through their obedient act of forgiveness, they were free. Often, this requires the person to forgive before any change in feelings.

How the offending party responds is not an indicator of whether or not you forgave. I'm amazed at how the offending party will sometimes justify their actions. Sometimes, they are incensed when they are told they are forgiven. As previously stated, don't confuse forgiveness with reconciliation. You have forgiven them. How they respond is not your concern.

FORGIVENESS PRAYERS

Prayer asking God to bring to mind all those you need to forgive:

Dear heavenly Father, I repent of holding onto anger and unforgiveness. I choose to forgive all who have wronged me in any way. Please bring to mind all the people whom I need to forgive. In Jesus' Name.

For every painful memory that God reveals for each person on your list, pray as follows:

Dear heavenly Father, I choose to forgive _____
[name the person] for _____ [what they did or failed to do] because it made me feel _____
[share the painful feelings, for example, rejected, dirty, worthless, or inferior].

After you have forgiven every person for every painful memory, then pray as follows:

Lord Jesus, in accordance with your Word, I choose to forgive _____ [insert the name of the offending party] for _____ [insert all things for which you need to forgive]. I release them to your love and mercy now in Jesus' Name.

These are sample prayers. Feel free to modify the wording as you see fit.

Forgiving Yourself

Earlier, I wrote about my wife Joanie's car accident. She knew that the accident was her fault. She looked at the turmoil the accident caused her, me, our children, and those around us. She knew that those around her and God would forgive her. But she also knew that she had to forgive herself. That was the only struggle she had throughout the entire ordeal. How do you forgive yourself when you know it's your fault? Why does it matter?

It matters because not forgiving yourself is to forsake the mercy and forgiveness of our Lord. Holding onto the guilt, the regret, is subjecting yourself to the enemy's condemnation. People sometimes condemn themselves because they feel like they are performing some weird form of penance. People sometimes think that if they chastise themselves enough, they won't do it again. I believe in learning from our mistakes, but it is unnecessary and unhealthy to wallow in regret and condemnation. Joanie had to forgive herself, and knowing that God was merciful helped. It also helped that all of us not only forgave her, but we also encouraged her to let it go.

Too many people in the Body of Christ believe God won't help them if they mess up. I realized years ago that if I have to do everything right for God to bless me, I might as well quit now. You, me, and everyone on this planet are incapable of doing everything right. I'm not justifying a sloppy lifestyle, but the truth is, at times, we will do something stupid. All of us will. And we need to know that the mercy of God is sufficient to free us from our mistakes.

Joanie forgave herself, realizing that while what she did was wrong, God still loved her; the blood of Jesus still cleanses her. She learned from this and moved on. From that point on, she believed she was going to get well.

Over the next few days, the doctors would come by with their latest findings. One diagnosis was that she damaged her knee (they misread the X-ray). Their report said that she fractured her spine and would never be without pain. Joanie thanked them, but none of that deterred her from believing she would be fine. To this day, she won't tell me some of the things the doctors said. She respected the doctors, but ultimately, she trusted the great physician.

My wife was completely healed. The four pelvic fractures lined up, so she didn't need surgery or a cast. Everything else healed on its own. She needed weeks of physical therapy but was back at work eleven weeks after her accident, on her feet all day, teaching middle school. As I write this, many years later, it is as if the accident never happened. God is faithful.

There is a false teaching known as hyper-grace. It says that Jesus paid for all of your sins, so it doesn't matter how you live. That's ridiculous. Jesus paid for all our sins, past, present, and future. His sacrifice on the cross frees believers from the power of sin. While we are free from sin, we are not free to sin. The wages of sin are still death (Rom 6:23). Persisting in a sinful lifestyle has consequences.

On the other hand, we live in a fallen world, and we all make mistakes. I have ministered to countless people who continued to beat themselves up over mistakes they made years ago. Doing that does not result in freedom. The Bible says,

> If we say that we have no sin, we are deceiving ourselves and the truth is not in us. If we confess our sins, he is faithful and righteous, so that he will forgive us our sins and cleanse us from all unrighteousness. If we say that we

have not sinned, we make him a liar and his word is not in us. (1 John 1:8-10)

It's important to be honest about mistakes or sins when they are committed. Freedom from sin requires confessing it, but it does not require wallowing in it. Self-abasement may appear noble, but it's playing right into the hands of the enemy. It denies the power of the blood of Jesus to cleanse us completely (Heb 9:13-14). There is no condemnation to those who are in Christ Jesus (Rom 8:1). As the saying goes, "cut yourself some slack," learn from the situation and move on.

The story of David and Bathsheba in 2 Samuel 11 highlights the mercy of God on a righteous man who sins. David has an affair with Bathsheba, and she becomes pregnant. Not wanting to be discovered, David calls for Bathsheba's husband, Uriah, to come home from the front lines of battle and spend some time with her. David hopes Uriah will have sex with his wife, thereby hiding David's sin. Instead of sleeping with his wife, Uriah responds to the call of his suffering soldiers and refuses to enter his house. David then tells Joab, the army commander, to put Uriah on the front line and withdraw from him, intending to kill Uriah. Joab does this, and Uriah is killed. David hides his sin, the sin of adultery and murder, until Nathan, the prophet, comes to David and confronts him. In Psalm 51, David repents before the Lord. The evil David did had consequences, but God did not strike him, nor did he lose his kingdom.

The story of David and Bathsheba is a story of the mercy of God. God's mercies are new every morning (Lam 3:23). I love that Scripture. There are days I feel like I've exhausted the mercy of God, but it's comforting to know that every morning there is a new supply of his mercy.

FORGIVING GOD

Forgiving others is based on how we perceive their actions. In many cases, it is obvious that we were wronged. Other times, there is a perception that we were wronged. This is more common when the offense happened when we were young. Children whose parents died when they were young sometimes need to forgive their parents for abandoning them. As adults, we understand that premature death is not abandonment. The wound, however, was sustained while the individual was a child based on a child's understanding of the events. It is crucial to respond based on that childlike understanding and forgive the adult who passed away.

The exception to this is when people harbor resentment and blame toward God and therefore feel the need to forgive him. This is a bad practice. People do hurt other people and need forgiveness. God never needs forgiveness. He is perfect. When someone feels that God let them down due to unfulfilled expectations, it is because of a lack of understanding. God is a perfect father who will never treat his children in a manner that is not loving or correct. God cannot lie; he is always faithful. A God who needs forgiveness is an imperfect being. Forgiving God means that we believe we have the right to judge him as unfaithful. This is a dangerous mindset. The truth is what brings freedom. A God who needs forgiveness is not truth.

God never needs forgiveness.
He is perfect.

We find a classic case of blaming God in everybody's favorite book, Job (I like the book of Job. It contains some great sarcasm which is my love language).

The overall theme of the book addresses the question of why the righteous suffer. I've heard people try to determine how Job was responsible for what happened and how we can learn from his mistakes so that we won't have to suffer. This misses the whole point of the book.

The story starts with the Lord saying to satan,[97] "Have you considered my servant Job? No one else on earth is like him, a man of perfect integrity, who fears God and turns away from evil" (Job 1:8). This is high praise for Job coming from God himself. God then allows satan to test Job, who loses his children and livestock. Job replies by saying, "Naked I came from my mother's womb, and naked I will leave this life. The Lord gives, and the Lord takes away. Blessed be the name of the Lord" (Job 1:21). The Bible says, "Throughout all this Job did not sin or blame God for anything" (Job 1:22). It is clear from what God has said that Job has behaved in an exemplary fashion despite what happened. This is confirmed in chapter 2. Satan is back again, and God's response to satan is,

> "Have you considered my servant Job? No one else on earth is like him, a man of perfect integrity, who fears God and turns away from evil. He still retains his integrity, even though you incited me against him, to destroy him for no good reason." (Job 2:3)

Satan is again given permission to test Job, this time afflicting him with boils over his entire body. Despite his suffering, Job continues to hold onto his integrity (Job 2:10).

Job's three friends, Eliphaz, Bildad, and Zophar, come to comfort Job. What follows is a discourse on how to not comfort your friend. Job, his three friends, and later Elihu spend the next thirty-five chapters going around and around trying to make sense

---

[97] *Satan* in Hebrew means adversary. It is not entirely clear if this is the devil or another adversary coming before the Lord. His name is not capitalized simply because I refuse to give him any dignity.

of what happened. It starts with Job mourning his very existence, "Why was I not stillborn; why didn't I die as I came from the womb?" (Job 3:11). Eliphaz responds by saying, "In my experience, those who plow injustice and those who sow trouble reap the same" (Job 4:8). Francis Anderson tells us that "Eliphaz goes too far. It is one thing to appeal to an abstract principle that seems self-evident to the mind of a man with moral sense. It is quite another to apply it to Job's particular case."[98] This is where Job's comforters go from comfort to judgment. Much of what they say is essentially, "We know God blesses the righteous and curses the wicked. We can look at you and figure out which one you are." Rather than comforting Job, they are trying to get Job to admit his guilt. In their minds, Job must be guilty; otherwise, this wouldn't have happened.

As the conversation ensues, they become more and more convinced of Job's guilt. In chapter 8, "Bildad the Shuhite replies, "How long will you go on saying these things? Your words are a blast of wind. Does God pervert justice? Does the Almighty pervert what is right? Since your children sinned against him, he gave them over to their rebellion" (Job 8:1-4). The more Job's friends speak of his guilt; the more Job defends himself. Job replies saying, "I am disgusted with my life. I will give vent to my complaint and speak in the bitterness of my soul. I will say to God, "Do not declare me guilty! Let me know why you prosecute me" (Job 10:1-2). Job later accuses God of depriving him of justice (Job 27:2).

The book of Job is forty-two chapters. Thirty-five chapters are dedicated to this verbal sparring between Job and his friends. That is over eighty percent of the book. At the end of their verbal wrangling, nothing is decided. They aren't even paying attention to each other but simply digging in their heels. Job's friends are convinced of Job's guilt. Job is convinced he is innocent and God has wronged him.

---

[98] Andersen, Francis I. 1976. *Job: An Introduction and Commentary.* Vol. 14. Tyndale Old Testament Commentaries. Downers Grove, IL: InterVarsity Press.

At the end of all this, God steps in and says to Job, "Who is this who obscures my counsel with ignorant words? Get ready to answer me like a man; when I question you, you will inform me" (Job 38:2-3). God is saying to Job, "OK, hotshot, let's see what you've got." For the next four chapters, God asks Job questions that Job can't answer. "Where were you when I established the earth? Tell me, if you have understanding. Who fixed its dimensions? Certainly, you know! Who stretched a measuring line across it?" (Job 38:4-5). It's as if the two of them are in a boxing ring, and Job is constantly getting peppered with jabs.

When God is done, Job responds by saying, "I know that you can do anything, and no plan of yours can be thwarted. You asked, who is this who conceals my counsel with ignorance? Surely, I spoke about things I did not understand, things too wondrous for me to know" (Job 42:2-3). Essentially, Job is admitting that he is in no position to judge God; in the grand scheme of things, he is clueless. He concludes by saying, "You said, listen now, and I will speak. When I question you, you will inform me. I had heard reports about you, but now my eyes have seen you. Therefore, I reject my words and am sorry for them; I am dust and ashes" (Job 42:4-6). God's response to his friends is, "you have not spoken the truth about me, as my servant Job has" (Job 42:7). Job has finally gotten it right.

The key to all of this is in verses 2 through 6. Job is admitting that he had no idea what was going on. But now he has seen God (verse 5), and in seeing God, he has come face to face with the one who is perfect in all his ways.

There are times when we are looking for answers, and there aren't any. In these times, we don't need answers. What we need is to see God for who he is. When we gaze into the face of the Perfect One, all fears and questions fade away. Freedom is not found in a concept or an idea. Freedom is found in a person.

***When we gaze into the face
of the Perfect One,
all fears and questions fade away.***

This is particularly important when a tragedy strikes. Often people are tempted to blame God. Where was God? Why didn't he answer me? While we should never accuse God, it is perfectly acceptable to ask him where he was, not in a condemnatory manner but from someone needing comfort. When tragedy strikes, it is not the time for needless speculation. People don't need a theological discourse. They need the comfort and love of our heavenly Father. If we turn to him, He will comfort us with a "peace that passes all understanding" (Phil 4:7).

FATHER WOUNDS

Growing up, I had a good father. While he wasn't always easy to live with, I knew he loved me. My father grew up poor during the depression and went to work at sixteen to support his family. As a result, he placed a high priority on providing for us. That was one of the primary ways he showed his love.

When I accepted Jesus as Lord, I had no problem interacting with Father God. I never struggled to know God was a good father, largely because of my earthly father's example.

Sadly, that is not always the case. Many people grow up in homes without a father. In some cases, the children never knew their father as he either died before they were born or he abandoned the family. Worse yet are those who grow up in households where they sustained abuse at their father's hand.

Father wounds are particularly damaging. Earthly fathers are to train their children, provide for their needs and provide a sense of security to help shape their character. When that is missing, children grow up without a sense of security, leading to anxiety and fear. Children who grow up without a good earthly father grow up without a proper role model. I remember talking to my friend who was ministering inner healing to men in prison. He said, "It's all fatherlessness."

When children have an abusive father, they often are robbed of their childhood. When there is sexual abuse, one's identity and sense of value are stolen. Children look to their parents for love, acceptance, and validation. They believe what their parents tell them. Children who are treated as a bother, as worthless, as no good, see themselves in that light and oftentimes grow up believing they have little or no value. It is common for those who have been victimized by sexual abuse to later become sexually promiscuous in an attempt to regain what was stolen. Instead of finding love, it simply results in more bondage. No amount of human wisdom or counseling can undo the damage. Therapy can help, but only God can free someone who has been sexually abused and restore their purity.

Father wounds often hinder one's relationship with God. Christians who have been wounded by their earthly fathers typically have a very difficult time relating to their heavenly Father. Almost every person I have ministered inner healing to projects their relationship with their earthly father onto their heavenly Father. They may be saved and love Jesus, but if they have been hurt by their earthly father, they typically have little or no fellowship with God the Father. Early in my Christian walk, I would try to help these people by teaching them what the Bible had to say regarding their heavenly Father. Having a good, biblical understanding of our heavenly Father is important. But they were rarely set free by my teaching alone.[99] They needed something more.

The Father Ladder is a tool developed by Dawna Desilva and Teresa Liebscher, co-founders of the Bethel *Sozo* inner healing ministry, Bethel Church, Redding, CA. The *Sozo* Training Manual explains, "when our family members do not understand or are unable to fulfill their roles in our lives, we have a misunderstood view of Father God, Jesus, and Holy Spirit."[100] The following is adapted from the Father Ladder tool.[101]

---

[99] While teaching didn't by itself set people free, it is of paramount importance in maintaining and increasing freedom.

[100] Dawna DeSilva, and Teresa Liebscher, *Bethel Sozo Ministry, Bethel Transformation Training Manual Basic Sozo*, (Redding, CA, 2011), 33.

[101] The *Sozo* model expands the use of the Father Ladder to Jesus and the Holy Spirit. It states that people project their relationship with friends and siblings onto Jesus and also project their relationship with their mother onto the Holy

The first step in getting free from father wounds is to forgive your earthly father and father figures if appropriate. This is an area where perception is reality. Even if the recollection of the earthly father was not accurate, or the circumstances were beyond his control, it is still essential to forgive him. I have ministered to people who grew up without a father simply because their father died when they were young or before they were born. Clearly, this is not their father's fault. However, the person did grow up without the care and protection they needed from an earthly father. Explaining why it wasn't their father's fault doesn't bring freedom but forgiving their father does.

As I wrote earlier, when we forgive, it is important to not minimize what happened. If someone's earthly father died before they were born and the person receiving ministry felt abandoned by that, I would still lead the person in a prayer of forgiveness. While it wasn't the father's fault, the person receiving ministry did experience abandonment. The prayer would be, "I choose to forgive my earthly father for not being there for me, for not providing the care, the support, the protection that I needed." Include everything that was lost due to your father's absence. If sexual abuse is involved, I would include forgiveness for your father stealing your purity and innocence, and for not treating you as valuable. In cases where there is deep wounding, it is tempting to ignore the areas of greatest hurt. Please don't do that. Allow the Holy Spirit to go deep. This is an opportunity to release years of hurt, of anguish. Don't be afraid of being honest. God's heart is for your freedom. This is where inner healing can feel like major surgery, cutting deep. As you work through this, allow the Holy Spirit to comfort you, bringing healing to your soul.

Where the father has been abusive, there are often additional wounds from the person's mother, sibling, friends, or relatives. This

---

Spirit. While I have found little correlation with Jesus and the Holy Spirit, there may be times when it is worth exploring.

is when the other family members knew about the abuse but did not stop it. In these cases, prayers of forgiveness are required for those who didn't protect the abused person.

Forgiving people in these circumstances can be difficult. It seems unfair to forgive those who mistreated you. Forgiving them can feel as if they are getting away with what they have done. This is not true. Forgiveness does not let them off the hook. It frees you from what happened. The grace of God is available to help you forgive. Don't let your feelings get in the way of forgiveness. We forgive as an act of our will, not because we feel like it.

Forgiveness paves the way to reestablish our intimacy with our Heavenly Father. In many cases, I would lead the person in a prayer where they would say one or more of the following:

"Father, I hand this to you. What do you have for me in return?"

"Father, are there any lies I'm believing about you?"[102] If he reveals any, I would have the person say, "Father, I renounce the lie that_____. I hand you this lie. Father, what is the truth?" I would then have them sit quietly until they heard from the Father.

There is no magic to the specific words or phrases. These are merely example prayers. Prayers in agreement with God's Word and from the heart are what matter.

I ministered to Beverly,[103] who was sexually abused by her father from the time she was young. When she came to me, she had

---

[102] Most lies are an attack on our identity or God's identity such as: I'm not good enough, I'm stupid, I'm a failure, I've made so many mistakes my life can't be fixed, No one loves me, No one understands me, God doesn't love me, God doesn't care about me, God can't be trusted.

[103] In all the stories, the names and details of the story have been changed to protect anonymity. The details of the encounters, conversations with God are accurate.

accepted Jesus but was still plagued because of the sexual abuse. I began the session by asking her to close her eyes and picture Father God. She could barely see him. He was far away in a mist. I then asked her to tell me about her earthly father. He was abusive, both verbally and sexually. Beverly understood that she needed to forgive him if she was going to be free. She forgave her dad. She then forgave her mom for not stopping her father from abusing her. When we were done forgiving all involved, I asked her to picture Father God again. To her amazement, he was now standing in front of her, and she could see him clearly. The conversation continued.

Me - "What do you see?"

Beverly - "He (Father God) is standing in front of me."

Me - "What does he look like."

Beverly - "He has a smile on his face, and his arms are stretched out towards me."

Me - "What do you want to do?"

Beverly - "I want to run into his arms. Can I do that?"

Me - "Ask him."

Beverly - "He said yes."

Me - "Go run towards him and tell me what happens."

Beverly - "I ran towards him, and he is hugging me."

Me - "What are you doing?"

Beverly - "I'm hugging him back."

Me - "How does it feel?"

Beverly - "It feels wonderful."

Me - "Ask him what he thinks of you."

Beverly - "He is whispering in my ear, and he tells me he loves me and I'm his precious daughter."

Me - "How does that feel? Does it feel real?"

Beverly - "Yes."

Me - "How does it feel to be in his arms?"

Beverly - "It feels safe. Like I never want to leave."

Me - "Ask him if you can come back. Let me know what he says."

Beverly - "He says I can come back anytime I want."

Me - "How does that feel?"

Beverly - "It feels wonderful."

This entire exchange took less than an hour. In that time, God freed Beverly from the bondage she was living in as a result of her father's abuse. The guilt and shame were gone. Father God went from scary to a loving father. As incredible as this sounds, this type of encounter with God is not unusual in an inner healing session. His heart is for freedom, and he sent Jesus to the cross to pay the penalty for our sins to purchase our freedom.

Janet was a woman who came to receive healing. She also was sexually abused by her father. As a result of the abuse, she became sexually promiscuous. Since that time, she accepted Jesus as her Lord and Savior and married a godly man. During her session, Janet forgave her father and was set free from the sexual abuse. She still struggled with guilt and shame due to her promiscuity. She felt that she was "damaged goods" and that her husband deserved someone better.

I told her, "Ask father God if he will restore your purity."

She asked him, and I saw a smile come across her face.

Me - "What did he say?"

Janet - "He said, 'Yes.'"

Me - "Ask him when he is going to restore it."

She closed her eyes and asked him. A big smile came across her face. She looked up at me and said, "He already has."

You may wonder why I had her ask God a question when I already knew the answer. The reason is simple. If the person being ministered to hears the answer from God, it is much more powerful than if they hear it from me. Hearing it from God directly also increases their confidence that they can hear his voice.

Exchanges between the person receiving ministry and the Trinity are the essence of inner healing. The tools and the methods are all designed to help walk the individual through a conversation with God. God (Father, Son, Holy Spirit) is the healer. Once connections with the Trinity are restored, healing flows.

While the Father Ladder is typically used when ministering to an individual, it can be applied to your own personal walk. The steps are as follows:

- Forgive your earthly father and any father figures. This could include relatives, step-fathers or others who filled that role.

- If abuse is involved and other family members did nothing to stop it, you may need to forgive them for not stepping in.

- Once you forgive your earthly father, pray: "Father, I hand you the lie that you are at all like my earthly father. Father, what is the truth?" Then listen quietly for his response.

- Often it is helpful to ask God, "What do you think of me?" Or "Are there any lies I'm believing about you?" Again, listen to hear what he is saying.

Write down the good things that father God says and make it a point to meditate on these truths. As you meditate on these truths, you will become more truth conscious and less susceptible to the enemy's lies.

Eliminating Access Points

"The whole world is under the sway of the evil one" (1 John 5:19). All around us are the trappings that accompany the evil around us. Satan is described as the "god of this age" (2 Cor 4:4). We are in the world but not of it (John 17:16-18). No one is immune from the woundings that plague this world.

Even though believers are free from the power of sin (Rom 6:6,7), they are still free to sin. The wages of sin is still death (Rom 6:23). Engaging in sin, whether intentionally or through ignorance, has consequences. Unhealthy choices result in an unhealthy life.

To get free, it is necessary to identify access points, places where the enemy has been granted access, either through sin or ignorance. Once these access points are identified, the next step is repentance (change) which allows God to bring healing to any wounds that have been sustained. To stay free, a person must permanently close the doors to these areas.

Several years ago, five of my friends and I went out for an evening of fellowship. We went to a local restaurant and shared several appetizers (women eat salads, men eat bacon). The menu listed the calories for each of these appetizers, which resulted in a caloric consumption of over two thousand calories per person (so much for guilt-free snacking). One of the guys decided that 12,000 calories of fat and carbs weren't enough, so he ordered dessert for us. To say that this was a large dessert was an understatement. It may have been more accurate to say that if properly distributed, this dessert could end world hunger. I remember watching him gorge himself on this, remarking, "I'm going to have to spend some extra time on the treadmill tomorrow to make up for this." The reality is, he could have spent most of the next day on the treadmill, and he still wouldn't burn all of the calories he consumed. It would have been much easier and much healthier to simply not consume all of that food.

Similarly, ingesting food, thoughts, mindsets, and unhealthy beliefs creates unnecessary struggles. Freedom requires us to close the doors of our mind and heart to harmful things. Fear is a significant impediment to many. If you are struggling with fear and are watching horror movies because you like them, then stop. You can't mentally consume media designed to scare you and live free from fear. There is an old saying, "You are what you eat." It is not only true physically. It is also true emotionally and spiritually.

The Four Doors

Many inner healing models address identifying and closing access points. Neil Anderson has *"Steps to Freedom in Christ."*[104] Here, the person receiving ministry is walked through seven steps, identifying areas where the enemy has gained access. The individual then repents of their part in these activities, finding freedom.

Another tool is the Four Doors. The Four Doors is a tool initially developed by Pablo Botari. It operates on the premise that the enemy gains access through four doors. The Four Doors was adapted for inner healing as part of the *Sozo* Inner Healing Model.[105] As the client is led through each door, the Holy Spirit reveals any root issues within these arenas. The person receiving ministry is guided through a process where lies are renounced, truth is discovered and embraced, and healing results. I have used

---

[104] Anderson, Neil T., *The Steps to Freedom in Christ: A Biblical Guide to Help You Resolve Personal and Spiritual Conflicts and Become a Fruitful Disciple of Jesus*, (Bloomington, MN: Bethany House Publishers, 2017), Kindle.
[105] DeSilva, Liebscher, *Sozo*, 39.

this tool many times and have seen God free people from bondages that have plagued them for years. The four doors are:[106]

Fear door: Inside this door is found worry, unbelief, the need for control, anxiety, isolation, apathy, and drug and alcohol addictions.

Hatred door: Inside this door are bitterness, envy, gossip, slander, anger, and self-hatred (low self-worth).

Sexual sin door: Inside this door are adultery, pornography, fornication, lewdness, molestation, fantasy, rape, and entertaining lustful thoughts.

Occult door: Inside this door is astrology, fortune-telling, tarot cards, séances, Ouija boards, manipulation, participation in covens, casting curses, and witchcraft practices.

In inner healing sessions, I often address rejection, generational (inherited) dysfunction, and shame as additional doors. I will discuss them in more detail in another section. While the specific nature of the wound may differ, the overall process is similar.

While the Four Doors is a tool I often use in ministering to others, it is easily adapted for someone to use for themselves. There are two ways to do this. One way would be to look at each door and ask the Lord if any of those attributes exist in your life. For example, you could ask the Lord, "Do I have any fear attributes, such as worry, unbelief, etc., in my life?" You would then wait to hear from the Lord. If the Lord says no, then move on to the next door. If he shows you that you have any of these, then the next move would be to ask him where it started. By going back to where it began, the root issue is revealed. Very often, when the root issue is resolved, the door closes. Other times, there may be more items to address, but once the root is removed, the rest are typically easy to deal with.

---

[106] DeSilva, Liebscher, *Sozo*, 39.

Once the root issue is identified, I recommend the following process:

- If there are other people involved, forgive them.

- Repent of any activity you had regarding this. For example, if he shows you worry, repent of worrying.

- Once you repent, ask him to show you the truth. This is important. It is the truth that sets us free (Jn 8:32). Once he reveals the truth, write it down and meditate on it.

- Ask him if there is anything else behind that door. Repeat the process until you are done.

This is repeated for all four doors.

You can go through the list and identify any areas you struggle with.

You can ask the Lord if any of these doors are open. If you sense or hear a "yes," ask him when it started.

A different approach to finding the access points, which I typically employ, is to ask the person to picture a door. For example, if we are going through the fear door, I would say, "Picture a door of fear." I would then ask them what they saw. Is the door open, is it closed, is it dark, is light coming from it? If the door is closed and there is no light, we move on. Otherwise, I have them ask God[107] what is behind the door. Once they identify that, I use the same process outlined above to bring freedom.

---

[107] In an inner healing session, I ask the person which member of the Trinity they are most comfortable with. This is especially important for those who have sustained wounds from their earthly father. I would then have them ask that specific member of the Trinity (Father God, Jesus or Holy Spirit) as I progress through the doors.

The visualization method may seem strange. However, all we are doing is communicating with God through pictures rather than words. It is clear from the Bible that God speaks in many ways: through his Word, prophecy, dreams, visions, angelic appearances, etc. Having people picture the door keeps them from being too analytical about the process. The goal is to let God identify where the door is open. The visualization method helps people focus on what Jesus is saying. If you are not comfortable with the visualization method, use one of the other methods.

It is essential you trust what he is showing you. He knows where and when the problem started. This is especially true of the occult door. It is not unusual to find that occult activity has been in someone's family for several generations. If the Lord shows you that, forgive the people involved, and renounce the activity.

Timothy scheduled an inner healing session at the recommendation of his wife. He indicated that he was struggling with heaviness and depression. During the session, Timothy and the team discovered that the heaviness he was experiencing resulted from occult activity in his family several generations in the past. Timothy was completely unaware of this. Interestingly, his wife had been suffering from a fear of the occult, even though she was unaware that this existed in Timothy's family. The occult activity surfaced as the team and Timothy proceeded through the Four Doors, specifically the door of the occult.

When questioned about this, Timothy's response was, "I wasn't aware of the occult that came out in the meeting, and I guess Jesus revealed that to me." He said he saw what he described as "vivid pictures" identifying freemason activity in his family's past. In addition, he related his experience as follows:

One of the images that kept flashing out, which is an image of 666, and on a poster had red lettering with 666 and basically an image of satan underneath that in black and red. That kept coming up as well, and I guess that was something that caught me by surprise. Anyway, we worked through that, which is good.

He said that seeing these pictures "was shocking" as he had no idea this existed.

As he worked through this with the team, he was freed from this activity and the heaviness he was experiencing. He remarked:

It was really through the prayer, the acknowledgment of it, and then Jesus closing the door, so it was a process. That process was finished with the sealing of the door. I felt freedom, a lifting of the heaviness, which was an acknowledgment of what happened.

One of the team members commented, "I remember as he left, he left with such an unburdened attitude."[108] Going through each of the Four Doors or other similar approaches, helps to identify the lies people believe. As the lies are replaced with truth, the access points are closed, and freedom results.

GENERATIONAL (INHERITED) DYSFUNCTION

I believe in free will. We are not robots. While God is sovereign, we are given certain choices. Deuteronomy 30:19-20 says,

I call heaven and earth to witness against you today, that I have set before you life and death, the blessing and the curse. So choose life in order that you may live, you and your descendants, by loving the Lord your God, by obeying his voice, and by holding fast to him; for this is your life and the length of your days, that you may live in the land

[108] Geoff Wattoff, April 2015, *An Evaluation of the Sozo Inner Healing Model In the Context of a Local Church,* diss., United Theological Seminary, 172.

which the Lord swore to your fathers, to Abraham, Isaac, and Jacob, to give them. (NASB)

God has given mankind a choice, just as he gave the children of Israel a choice. They could choose life or death, the blessing or the curse. The way that they (and we) choose life is by choosing to walk with God.

While we have choices, it is also apparent that free will has certain limitations. None of us chose where we were born. None of us chose our parents. I was born in Brooklyn, New York, to George and Marion Wattoff. I didn't get a say in that matter. I grew to the towering height of 5'8". I wanted to be 6'2," but given my genetics, that wasn't going to happen, no matter how hard I tried. I have blue eyes. I was naturally good at math and science and bad at art (I am the only person I know who actually failed art in eighth grade). While my efforts (or lack thereof) had a part in my development, I was never going to be an NBA basketball player or an all-pro linebacker.

In addition to genetics, certain environmental factors shaped my development. I'm Jewish, which comes with its own set of cultural mores. My parents stressed education. For me, college was never a choice; it was a given I was going. I was taught to work hard and to be respectful. While I wouldn't call my family religious, we all believed in a good God. I went to Hebrew school for three years and was Bar Mitzvah'ed. All of this left an imprint on my heart and mind.

None of us were raised in a perfectly antiseptic environment. We all were raised in an environment that profoundly impacted our upbringing. I can't remember the number of people I've encountered over the years who were raised in dysfunctional families. Sexual abuse, alcoholism, drug abuse, and violence are all too common. These experiences leave an impression on our hearts and minds. It shapes the way we think, the way we view the world, and the way we view ourselves and God.

When we accept Jesus as Lord, the Bible tells us we become new creations in Christ. The old things have passed away, and new things have come (2 Cor 5:17). God takes out the old heart of stone and gives us a new heart (Ezek 36:26-27). We pass from death to life, from the kingdom of darkness to the kingdom of God (Col 1:13-14). We are declared righteous (2 Cor 5:21) and adopted into the family of God as sons and daughters (Rom 8:15-17). Everything is now perfect. Or is it?

When I got saved, certain things from my past just fell off. I stopped lying. Before I accepted Jesus, I had no problem with lying. After I got saved, it stopped. I don't ever remember consciously repenting over it, nor do I remember making a decision to stop. It just happened. Other things seemed to wither and die. They didn't immediately change, but over time they just stopped operating in my life.

Some traits seemed to hang on for dear life. These were stubborn. I would pray and repent, but I had difficulty getting rid of these mindsets and these practices in my life. I knew they were wrong, but somehow, they held on.

What I have described is not unique to me. It is the experience of everyone I have ever ministered inner healing to. It is also the experience of everyone I ever spoke to regarding this. Some things fall off, while some things are stubborn.

Some of our traits are inherited. Some are the result of our upbringing. I got a strong work ethic from my father. I also inherited his fear of money. He never verbalized it, but he modeled it for me. He grew up poor and made a good living. However, he would wake up from nightmares that he was poor and living back in Brooklyn (which represented poverty to him). While I didn't find out about this until after he passed away, it was in the atmosphere of our home, and I caught it. I didn't know I caught it until I married, and money was tight. I was shocked about how I reacted. I was almost paralyzed with a fear of going broke.

There is a lot of debate about what is often called generational curses. Some people say they are biblical. Others say that all of that is broken off when you are saved. Craig Keener, a top scholar, has good insight into this issue:

> Again granted, a concept such as "generational curses" may have some biblical precedent. Children often walk in their parents' behavior (e.g., Gn 12:13; 20:2; 26:7), and walking in the ways of our ancestors can reap their blessings or judgments (e.g., Ex 20:5–6; Dt 5:9–10; 7:9). Nor do I deny that practitioners are often, probably usually, sincere, and that God often responds to a misinformed but sincere heart. But the biblically specified solution to ancestral disobedience is not a prominent preacher's formulaic prayer of deliverance; it is turning from the ways of our ancestors to obey God's word. This recognition invites teaching about how to recognize inherited familial and cultural sins and how to turn from them, not consumer-sanitized and-packaged crisis experiences.[109]

While I agree with Keener, generational issues can be challenging to identify. What appears normal to us, especially if it has been in our family lineage for a long time, may actually be dysfunctional. I have a friend who always seemed to have a hair-trigger temper. He loves God, but it seems that anything would set him off. I remember talking to him about it, and his reply was, "I'm just a

---

[109] Craig S. Keener, *Spirit Hermeneutics: Reading Scripture in Light of Pentecost* (Grand Rapids, MI: William B. Eerdmans Publishing Company, 2016), 271.
Note: While I agree with his assessment, I have seen people set free as a result of what he calls "a formulaic prayer of deliverance." At the same time, my experience is that this is the exception and not the norm.

hard-headed _____." He was raised in an atmosphere where everyone acted like that. All his relatives were like that. To him, it was normal. His response indicated that he accepted it as who he was. It was his identity. I remember telling him that it might have been in his earthly lineage, but it was not who he was in Christ. Our heavenly Father doesn't have a temper. He doesn't fly off the handle. He is patient and kind.

My heritage is as a Russian Jew. Some of my habits and mindsets reflect that heritage. There is nothing wrong with that. In some ways, our differing heritages create a diversity that reflects God's creativity. However, I am also a child of God, and it is of paramount importance that I allow my heavenly identity to take priority over my earthly identity. My identity as his son, as his child, and as his heir is how I see myself. It can take time to renew our minds to our kingdom heritage, but it brings freedom. Sanctification (being set apart) is progressive. Part of the process is getting rid of the stubborn crud, those negative traits accumulated from our past that we bring into the kingdom of God. The key to getting free is to identify the root issue. When did this start?

> *It is of paramount importance that*
> *I allow my heavenly identity to take priority*
> *over my earthly identity.*

Generational stuff are areas where the enemy has been given access. This is where we need to rely on the Holy Spirit. Sometimes the person being ministered to knows where the root is. Most of the time, they do not know, but God does, and he wants us free. If we simply rely on the Holy Spirit, ask him and wait for an answer; he will reveal it to us. What he reveals may seem unrelated to our struggle. Trust him and walk through the process outlined in the Four Doors.

Helen came to the church to support her friend's inner healing. She did not intend to have her own inner healing session. However, God had other plans.

The night Helen and her friends arrived at the church was unusually chaotic. Members of the church were busy loading cartons full of shoeboxes into trucks for Operation Christmas Child, a ministry of Samaritan's Purse. People were busy building sets for the upcoming Christmas play. Others were rehearsing for the play. That night was also intercessory prayer night at the church. When Helen and her friends arrived, they were each handed a clipboard with the registration form and the pre-test survey for the inner healing session[110]. Not knowing the procedure and wanting to comply, they filled out the paperwork. They each received inner healing ministry.

During her session, Helen continued to experience greater freedom. One team member said, "We were having what I would call a textbook inner healing session." The team then moved to the door of sexual sin. Helen continued to participate. At that point, the team began to lead Helen in breaking soul ties.

A soul tie is an emotional connection between two people. Unholy soul ties can happen when a sinful sexual relationship, such as adultery or sex outside of marriage exists. For the person to become whole, they must sever these soul ties. The team sensed that for Helen to be set free, it was necessary to break soul ties that were formed due to sexual sin. As the team walked Helen through the breaking of soul ties, the mood in the room shifted. Helen went from cooperative to unresponsive. [111]

---

[110] Pre-test surveys were only used when I was collecting data for my dissertation.
[111] Breaking a soul tie can be done with a three-part prayer. The first part is to repent. "Father, I repent of an ungodly soul tie with (person's name). The second part is to forgive the person involved. "Father, I forgive (person's name) for their involvement with me in this sin. The third part is to break the soul tie. "Father, I

Rachel, who was conducting the inner healing session as first chair,[112] recalls what happened when they began to break soul ties:

That is when she shut down. Her eyelids fluttered a little, and she kept her eyes closed and was unresponsive. I asked her if she was okay and some other things with no response. After a time of silence with Helen still unresponsive, we began to try to take authority over "it." What really started working was when Tony [the second chair] commanded a spirit to come out and said "come out in the name of Jesus." Several times Tony would say, "the blood of Jesus," and he would say come out, and she would shake her head, "no," and he would say, "yes, you will come out." At one point, she turned her back to him in the swivel chair, and he said, "You can't get away from Jesus." We told her to take authority over the spirit and advised her that it would be great if she could say the name of Jesus.

She bent over and cried a little and started to emerge as normal again. She asked me if we were done. I said, "We aren't holding you here, but we can continue if you want." She asked for paper and a pen and handed me a note that said, "Don't listen to me; I'm lying." So, we asked her to say the name of Jesus. As this occurred, she held her chest, saying it was hurting, and she also cried and said, "help me." Tony encouraged her, "It's okay, you're doing good,"

---

break this soul tie in the name of Jesus and I ask you to restore anything broken to each of us.

[112] It is common for two people (referred to as first chair and second chair) to be present to perform inner healing. The first chair interacts with the person receiving ministry. The second chair records the truths that God reveals, and gives them to the person receiving ministry at the end of the session. The second chair also will on occasion pass a note to the first chair if they sense something in their spirit that the first chair has not addressed. It is unusual for the roles to switch during a session. It was done in this session as Tony, the second chair had much more experience in deliverance.

and asked her to say Jesus is Lord. Finally, she was able to say it.

At this point, we led her through forgiveness over the man with the soul tie; this time, she could respond and speak. After this, we then moved to seal the door, and she could not. At this point, I asked if Jesus would help her, and he gave her a key. She was afraid to use the key, so I talked her through using the key, and then the door went away

Helen described the experience as follows:

I'm repeating the prayer with her [to break soul ties], and I couldn't hear her anymore. I couldn't finish the prayer because I felt like I was leaving my body, I couldn't see everything when my eyes were closed, but I could see the room, I could see what they were doing, I could see everything that was happening and I could no longer speak.

I had no control of my body, and deep down, I was crying and screaming for help. I was trying to say Jesus' name, and I couldn't say his name at all. I was there trying to fight it, and at the same time, I was listening. They were talking to me, saying, "Helen, you are bigger, you are stronger than this, you have God, you have Jesus Christ," and I'm there responding in my mind, "Yes, I know," but I couldn't do anything about it.

The song "Break Every Chain" was just playing in my mind over and over; I don't know why. That was all I kept hearing: break every chain, break every chain, break every chain. Finally, after they kept praying, again and again, I could speak, and I opened my eyes. Then, I again felt like I had left my body, but my eyes were open this time, and they were talking to me but it was not me responding. I tried to tell them, "It's not me. . ." and I finally asked them for a piece of paper.

I wrote to them, and it was me saying, "Don't listen to what I am saying," because it wasn't me, and I didn't know if they knew that or not. I did not want to say everything that had been done to me, and I was not myself, but I wanted to be myself. I don't know if this makes sense.

I remember at one point, I looked at her [Rachel], and I cried. I wanted her to help me to keep praying and not believe that it was me responding. So after they prayed, at some point, I felt free again, but I did not know everything that had happened. This happens a lot, and I'm tired of that happening to me. I don't want this to happen to me anymore.

What happened was that Helen could no longer speak as she was being controlled by a demon. When she wrote on the paper, "Don't listen to what I am saying," it was Helen crying for help. Tony, who was in the session as the second chair, recounts the deliverance:

We just commanded the thing to go to and release her. The thing that seemed to be the key that had an effect on the demon was speaking about the blood of Jesus. I was saying, "The blood of Jesus is against you, the blood of Jesus, the blood of Jesus," and it [the demon] was getting more and more agitated until finally it or they left. Praise the Lord.

Eventually, the demon left, and Helen was set free. Afterward, she was interviewed, and during this time, she said, "I feel light; nothing is weighing me down." As a result of the inner healing session, Helen is enjoying her relationship with God. She explains in her words,

I talk to God more now, and it's more like a relationship. I just don't talk to him when I pray. I just talk to him now . . . I can't believe what happened to me. I joke around with him. I depend on him more now, not just as God as like my father, my best friend.

In her interview, Helen was excited that she hears his voice much more clearly than before the inner healing session. As a result, she stated that she "realizes that's really him talking to me." Helen hears the voice of God more clearly, and the freedom she experiences has drastically altered how she views God and her understanding of what God thinks of her. She recounts that later in the inner healing session, following her deliverance:

There was a point when they [the inner healing team] asked me to ask God how he sees me. He showed me a trophy in a glass trophy case, and it was so big, clean, beautiful, and sparkly that I'm so amazed by it sometimes that I marvel and even feel conceited. Or I will say to God, "No, that can't be true." But I have realized that's actually how he sees me, and to this day, I am amazed. What he thinks of me is what no other guy or person in the world could ever say about me, and it's just so amazing.

At the beginning of her session, when Helen was asked to picture father God, all she saw was a bright light. At the end of her session, the team once again asked Helen to picture the Father. This time she recounts,

I saw a warm light; it was very pleasing, and it was very relaxing and very peaceful. I could see arms stretching out wide open like I felt like he was saying, "I'm here, come, I'm right here."

And I felt so good, like my spirit felt so good, relaxed, and pleasing. It was like the perfect feeling. I thought it was a perfect feeling. I can't really describe in any other way that's how I felt.

Helen commented on her inner healing session. "It was very beneficial, it was very needed, it was very perfect timing . . . everything was perfect, it was perfect."

Most inner healing sessions are not as dramatic as Helen's. What is encouraging is that the Holy Spirit is eager to go deep, identify the heart of our dysfunction and bring healing. Nothing is beyond his reach.

OVERCOMING REJECTION

Rejection is another area where the enemy can gain access. Earlier in this book, I shared how God set me free from rejection. While many of you can draw some hope from my story, we are all different. The Little League vision I had may or may not speak to you. My journey is not your journey. But if you have accepted Jesus as your Lord and Savior, then my God is your God, and the God that set me free desires to set you free as well.

The pain of rejection is borne out of our need for acceptance. We are social creatures. We need to be loved, to be accepted. We need to know that we matter and that we are not just taking up space on planet earth. The reality is that as we journey through life on earth, some people will accept us, and some will not. The solution to overcoming rejection is not to learn how to get everyone to love you. That is an impossible, wearying task. Not everyone will love you if you are the authentic man, the authentic woman God made you to be. We have to accept that. That has nothing to do with us. If we look at the men and women in the Bible, not everyone loved them. Many of the greatest men and women of God in the Bible and throughout history endured significant opposition from people who opposed them. In the Sermon on the Mount, Jesus makes the following statement,

> You are blessed when they insult you and persecute you and falsely say every kind of evil against you because of me. Be glad and rejoice, because your reward is great in heaven. For that is how they persecuted the prophets who were before you. (Matt 5:11-12)

Years ago, I was slandered by certain members of a church. I remember going home and whining, as if I was telling the Lord, "They were mean to me." In response, I got this impression. It was as if the Lord was looking at me, giving me a thumbs up and saying, "Welcome to the club."

Some people attempt to avoid rejection by becoming a people pleaser, where everything they do is to try to gain the approval of others. This is an impossible task. Pleasing one person will, at times, automatically draw the ire of someone else. There are times when pleasing God results in displeasing people. Which one will you choose? The apostle Paul said, "For am I now trying to persuade people, or God? Or am I striving to please people? If I were still trying to please people, I would not be a servant of Christ" (Gal 1:10).

Joshua said it this way,

> But if it doesn't please you to worship the Lord, choose for yourselves today: Which will you worship—the gods your ancestors worshiped beyond the Euphrates River or the gods of the Amorites in whose land you are living? As for me and my family, we will worship the Lord. (Josh 24:15)

Choosing God, and saying "yes" to him, automatically means you are saying "no" to some others. There are times when God is the minority opinion. Jeremiah was the least popular of all the prophets in his day. The false prophets were far more accepted by the people because they told the people what they wanted to hear. Jeremiah wasn't motivated by that. He delivered the word of the Lord. We shouldn't be motivated to do something simply to gain the approval of people. Our motivation should be to please God.

There are times when God is the minority opinion.

People who wear masks in an effort to please others never experience acceptance, even if they achieve popularity. Deep down, they know that it is the fake version of them that is being accepted and not their authentic selves. The only way to escape all this is to be the authentic person God calls you to be.

Since it is impossible to entirely avoid rejection, the answer is to learn to not let it wound you. This can be especially difficult when you have been rejected by someone close to you or when you have been rejected in such a way as to bring public humiliation. You can't just shake off that level of pain. While you can't avoid rejection, you can live free from the wounds the rejection brings.

First and foremost, we need to know that we are loved and accepted by God. We are "remarkably and wondrously made" (Ps 139:14). We are "accepted in the beloved" (Eph 1:6 NKJV). The Bible says, "See what great love the Father has lavished on us, that we should be called children of God! And that is what we are. . ." (1 John 3:1 NIV). We are loved by God, accepted by God, valued and honored by God. We are handcrafted by our loving heavenly Father (Eph 2:10). The more we understand God's great love for us, the less people's rejection will affect us.

This understanding of our acceptance in Christ doesn't happen overnight. It doesn't come by attending one twelve-week course. It takes time sitting in his presence, experiencing his grace and his love. Learn to sit in his presence and be still (Ps 46:10), to feel his tender touch, to hear his loving voice. I am a great believer in studying the Bible, and in hiding his Word in our hearts. Lasting freedom doesn't come any other way. But there is more to this than simply quoting half a dozen Scriptures. The truths in the Bible are to be experienced.

Rejection is the enemy's tool to keep you from fully being the person God created you to be. It is an attack on authenticity. When we give in to rejection, we surrender to a lie, the lie that we are not valuable, not significant. We are telling God that he made a mistake when he made us.

We can never overcome rejection as long as we have an unhealthy need for acceptance. As long as we feel we need to be accepted by a specific person or group, we will compromise to gain their favor. If we are needy, we are saying that we need their acceptance and their approval to be of value. When we act from our place of neediness, we are operating from a lie and not the truth. Healing comes from the truth.

We are often attacked in our area of greatest strength or gifting. What was one thing (among many) that the Apostle Paul was known for? Revelations. Paul wrote a large portion of the New Testament. The revelation of who we are in Christ, the understanding of what Jesus did on the cross, and our standing before the Father as his righteous children are revealed primarily in Paul's letters. What caused the thorn in his flesh? Revelations. Paul was given a thorn in the flesh so that he wouldn't exalt himself due to his revelations (2 Cor 12:7). The enemy uses rejection to intimidate us and keep us from living in the fullness of who God created us to be.

> If anyone does not welcome you or listen to your words, shake the dust off your feet when you leave that house or town. Truly I tell you, it will be more tolerable on the day

of judgment for the land of Sodom and Gomorrah than for that town. (Matt 10:14-15)

If you are doing what God tells you to do and people reject you, that is on them, not you.

> **If you are doing what God
> tells you to do and people reject you,
> that is on them, not you.**

The wound of rejection, like all other wounds, can be healed. As I stated earlier, I often treat the wound of rejection as an additional door when taking someone through the Four Doors. Start by simply asking the Lord, "When did this start?" Let him take you back to that place. Don't try to find it on your own. Once he shows you do the following:

- Forgive anyone and everyone he brings to your mind.

- Renounce the lie of rejection. If there were specific lies that he reveals (such as the lie; "I'm not good enough, I'll never measure up, I'm too stupid") renounce those.

- Then pray, "God, I give you these lies. What is the truth?" Take the time to get quiet and listen. When he shows you the truth, write it down.

- Ask him if there are any other areas of rejection in your life. Continue to do this until you have uncovered all these other areas.

- Take time to meditate on the truths he has shown you. Continue to do that until all traces of rejection are gone.

Freedom from rejection doesn't always come within a single session like this. There are times when God will continue to reveal things to you. When he does, continue to follow the process. The process outlined in this book is a guide, not a step-by-step flowchart. Take the time to sit and commune with God as you go through the process. Resist the temptation to rush through it as a task you have to check off your to-do list. Healing comes from intimacy with him, not from following a set of rules.

As you go through the process, take the time to praise God for your freedom, even if it seems you are still struggling. Praise in the midst of difficulties is an act of faith that brings freedom. Paul and Silas praised God from the depths of a Philippian jail, and God sent an earthquake to free them (Acts 16:22-26). God instructed Jehoshaphat to praise God when attacked by three armies. God sent an ambush which caused Jehoshaphat's enemies to turn on each other and destroy each other (2 Chronicles 20). The Bible instructs us to "count it all joy" (James 1:2) in the midst of difficulties. As we praise God, we transfer our focus from ourselves to him, facilitating receiving from him.

SHAME

In place of your shame, you will have a double portion; in place of disgrace, they will rejoice over their share. So they will possess double in their land, and eternal joy will be theirs. (Isa 61:7)

Sam Storms defines shame as "a painful emotion caused by a consciousness of guilt, failure, or impropriety that often results in the paralyzing conviction or belief that one is worthless, of no value to others or to God, unacceptable, and altogether deserving of disdain and rejection."[113]

Christine Caine remarks, "Shame makes us feel small. Flawed. Not good enough. And controlled. Shame is the fear of being unworthy, adversely affecting our relationship with God, ourselves, and others. It greatly hinders our ability to receive God's unconditional love—and share it with others."[114]

It's clear that shame stands in the way of a healthy identity and a healthy soul. What makes shame so damaging is that it causes people to hide. Shame causes people to cover up, to pretend that those things that caused the shame don't exist. Ignoring shame doesn't make it go away. Shame starts a cycle of hiding and denial. Eventually, the hidden things manifest.

Shame was not part of God's plan for mankind. Before the fall, Adam and Eve lived without shame, even though they were naked (Gen 2:25). What happened?

---

[113] Sam Storms, *Understanding Spiritual Warfare*, (Grand Rapids, MI: Zondervan, 2021), p 190.
[114] Christine Caine, *Unashamed*, (Grand Rapids, MI: Zondervan, 2016), p 11.

The serpent deceived Eve into eating from the tree of the knowledge of good and evil, the one thing God commanded them not to do. Eve then gives the fruit to her husband, who also eats. The Bible tells us, "Then the eyes of both of them were opened, and they knew they were naked; so they sewed fig leaves together and made coverings for themselves" (Gen 3:7). Shame has now entered into Adam and Eve's world. Their shame caused them to hide from God (Gen 3:8). All the sin, suffering, and sickness in the world can be traced back to this event (see Rom 5:12). The good news is that Jesus' sacrifice was more potent than Adam's fall. The Bible declares, "If by the one man's trespass, death reigned through that one man, how much more will those who receive the overflow of grace and the gift of righteousness reign in life through the one man, Jesus Christ" (Rom 5:17).

THE EXTRAVAGANT FATHER

The parable that is commonly known as the Prodigal Son is found in Luke 15. As James Edwards points out, the distinctiveness of the parable lies in the father, not the son.

> The uniqueness of the parable does not consist in the sons, however. We all know people like the rebellious younger son or the resentful older one. At one time or another, in fact, most of us have been like the one or the other. But we have never known anyone like the father, nor would we claim to be such ourselves. The father is the first party named and the last to speak, the unique and causal figure in both halves of the parable. The relationship between the two sons has long eroded, as has their relationship to the family, although each in different ways. None of the problems posed in the parable can be solved without the father, who is the last remaining link of each son to the family. In varying ways, neither son's story is complete: we

are not told, for instance, how the younger son behaved once he was received back into the family; and more important, we are not told whether the older son overcame his resentment and joined the celebration. The father is the only finished character in the parable. He has done all that can and need be done to restore the family. The parable is about the indomitable love of the Father.[115]

In this parable, a father has two sons. The younger son asks the father for his share of the estate. This is a shameful request.

It is a certified public statement that he no longer wishes to live within or be identified by the family. In requesting what should become available only at his father's death, the son is, in effect, writing his father's death certificate. In ancient Jewish society, that was a virtually unforgivable offense[116]

The son is making it clear that he is cutting all ties with his family. He is disgracing his family, his father, and himself. This is heartbreaking for the father. It is clear from all this that the son doesn't care. He is turning his back on his family. He is venturing out into the world, planning to never return again.

The son ventures out into the world and squanders his share of the estate in riotous living. His circumstances are further affected by a famine in the land. He is now alone in a foreign land with no money, no means of support, and no family to help him. He is alone in every sense of the word. Out of desperation, he hires himself out to feed pigs. He is turning his back on his Jewish heritage. Edwards states that,

[115] James R. Edwards, *The Gospel according to Luke*, ed. D. A. Carson, The Pillar New Testament Commentary (Grand Rapids, MI; Cambridge, U.K.; Nottingham, England: William B. Eerdmans Publishing Company; Apollos, 2015), 437–438.

[116] Edwards, *The Gospel according to Luke*, Luke 15:11-32.

A Jew could be hired by a Gentile without violating dietary laws, and thus without defiling himself. The Greek *kollan* (v. 15) does not mean "hire," but "to bind oneself closely to another, unite with, cleave to." The boy must identify with "that country" in such a way that his Jewish identity is not only defiled but expunged[117]

He has now lost not only his family and his wealth but his dignity and his identity as well. The Bible says, "And he was longing to be fed with the pods that the pigs ate, and no one gave him anything" (Luke 15:16).

At this point, he "comes to his senses," realizing that his father's workers are living better than he is. He decides to go home, not as a son but as a worker. So devastating was his betrayal that he is convinced he has forfeited his right to be a family member. He decides, "I'll get up, go to my father, and say to him, "Father, I have sinned against heaven and in your sight. I'm no longer worthy to be called your son. Make me like one of your hired workers" (Luke 15:18,19).

Having reached his decision, the son heads home, hoping to find enough grace from his father to be treated as a hireling. But the father has other, far more gracious plans. While he is yet a long way from home, "his father saw him and was filled with compassion. He ran, threw his arms around his neck, and kissed him" (Luke 15:20b). Edwards, commenting on this, states,

> The father extends compassion and forgiveness not when he knows of his son's repentance, but when, for all he knows, he is still in the "far" country. Forgiveness is not merited by repentance, but freely and unconditionally bestowed upon his son before he says a word.[118]

---

[117] Edwards, *The Gospel according to Luke*, Luke 15:11-32.
[118] Edwards, *The Gospel according to Luke*, Luke 15:11-32.

There was no way for the father to know his son was coming home. He had to be waiting regularly, looking, hoping that his son would return.

The significance of the father running to meet his son cannot be overstated. The son coming home, walking down the road was the ultimate humiliation. He could feel the eyes of everyone in the village at him, judging him. He had rehearsed what he would say to his father, "Father, I have sinned against heaven and in your sight. I'm no longer worthy to be called your son" (v21).

The Bible tells us that "while the son was still a long way off, his father saw him and was filled with compassion. He ran, threw his arms around his neck, and kissed him" (v20). That act of compassion changed everything. By running out to meet his son, the father bore the son's shame. Kenneth Bailey comments, "It is his compassion that leads the father to race out to his son. He knows what his son will face in the village. He takes upon himself the shame and humiliation due the prodigal." [119] Instead of the son walking down the road alone, he walked with his father. Instead of shame, there was rejoicing. What did the son do to deserve such mercy? Absolutely nothing. The story of the prodigal son is really the story of the extravagant father who bore the son's shame so that the son could be restored.

It is hard to overestimate the father's actions. They live in a culture where honor is highly regarded, and shame is to be avoided at all costs. It's clear that, in this case, the father is not thinking about preserving his honor. He is focused on loving his son and restoring him to the family.

Despite the father's reaction, the son still doesn't seek restoration. He replies by saying, "Father, I have sinned against heaven and in

---

[119] Kenneth E. Bailey, *The Cross and the Prodigal: Luke 15 through the Eyes of Middle Eastern Peasants*, Second Edition. (Downers Grove, IL: IVP Books, 2005), 67.

your sight. I'm no longer worthy to be called your son," the very words he has been rehearsing. But these words don't even register on the father's conscience. The father replies by telling his servants,

> Quick! Bring out the best robe and put it on him; put a ring on his finger and sandals on his feet. Then bring the fattened calf and slaughter it, and let's celebrate with a feast, because this son of mine was dead and is alive again; he was lost and is found!" So they began to celebrate. (Luke 15:22-24)

Edwards notes,

> Robe, ring, and sandals—all three signify status, reputation, and honor.[120]

> These gestures far exceed the son's needs. The servants could have satisfied his needs, but only his father can rehabilitate him, and rehabilitation requires honor. The son may return as a slave, but he will not be received as one. The slaughter of a calf in a culture where meat was a rarity signals a celebration.[121]

I often wondered why the father put the ring and the robe on the son in his present condition. His contact with the pigs rendered him unclean. Putting the robe on him would have made it unclean, and they would have to burn it. Why waste a perfectly good robe? Why not wait until the son was cleaned up and then put the robe on him?

The reason goes back to the father's extravagant heart. The robe and the ring signified his standing in the family. The robe and the ring meant that he was a son. He didn't get reinstated in the family after he got cleaned up. He was always a son in the mind of the

---

[120] Edwards, *The Gospel according to Luke*, Luke 15:11-32.
[121] Edwards, *The Gospel according to Luke*, Luke 15:11-32.

father. He didn't become a son again when he came home. The entire time he was away from home, bringing shame to his family, he was still a son in his father's eyes. The son may have disowned his father, but the father never disowned the son.

This story is a magnificent picture of our Heavenly Father's extravagant love for us. In the garden, Adam and Eve sinned. However, God never stopped loving, never stopped pursuing mankind. And at the proper time, he sent his son. The Bible tells us,

> But when the set time had fully come, God sent his Son, born of a woman, born under the law, to redeem those under the law, that we might receive adoption to sonship. Because you are his sons, God sent the Spirit of his Son into our hearts, the Spirit who calls out, "Abba, Father." So you are no longer a slave, but God's child; and since you are his child, God has made you also an heir. (Gal 4:4-7)

We are not slaves. We don't have to earn our righteousness, our right standing with God. Jesus purchased our salvation and our freedom and gave them to us. Not only that, his sacrifice "cleansed our conscience from dead works" (Heb 9:14).

The shame we often battle is nothing more than an insidious lie from the pit of hell, designed to keep us in bondage. It makes us feel ashamed, dirty, and unworthy. The truth is that just as the prodigal son's father bore the son's shame, Jesus bore our shame.

I have ministered to countless men and women who love God but still bear the shame of bad choices in their past. Men and women who turned to drugs, alcohol, and sex to numb their pain. They then battle with the shame of their bad choices. They continually beat themselves up over what they've done, embarrassed to tell anyone when God has already dealt with their sin and shame.

Years ago, one of our deacons was struggling with an addiction to prescription painkillers. The doctor had prescribed them for his back pain. The pain was so intense that he kept taking them until he was addicted. I'll never forget the Sunday when God set him free. Our pastor looked at him and told him to let go of the shame. Once he realized he was forgiven, that God didn't see any shame, he could release it. As soon as the shame was gone, so was the addiction.

God knows about your sin before you confess it. Confession isn't to alert him to what you have done. Confessing your sin is for your cleansing. Jesus died for your sins past, present and future. He knew what you were going to do, and he went to the cross for you, not in spite of what you did but because of what you did. It's common to talk about salvation being a free gift. Milton Friedman, the famous economist, popularized the saying, "There is no such thing as a free lunch." In other words, someone is paying for it. Salvation was free for us, but it wasn't free. Someone had to pay the penalty for our sin. Someone had to bear our shame. It took a sinless man to do it. Jesus bore our sin, our dysfunction, and our shame as the greatest act of love ever recorded.

The first and most important step in overcoming shame is to recognize it for what it is. It is a cunning, treacherous lie designed to keep people in hiding. If you are struggling with shame, know that God is not ashamed of you. Jesus came and took your shame. The parable of the Extravagant Father (commonly known as the Prodigal Son) illustrates the lengths that God will go to rid you of your shame. All of your shame was canceled at the cross.

Salvation was free for us, but it wasn't free.

Shame is a lie. Once it is identified as a lie, the process to get free is the same as it is for any lie:

- Ask God if there are any other lies you believe.

- Ask him when the shame started.

- When he shows you when it began, forgive anyone involved with your shame.

- Hand him the shame. I typically lead people in a prayer that says, "Jesus, I hand you this shame. I renounce the lie that _____ (whatever he has shown you). Jesus, what's the truth? It's imperative that you hear the truth and continue to meditate on it after your session is over.

- Ask him if there is any other shame that you need to get rid of. Continue the process until the shame is gone.

Never forget that shame is a lie from hell. If you are feeling shame, recognize that the enemy is using shame to keep you from getting free. Don't let shame rule. You can live free from shame by bringing it out in the open and renouncing it.

SECTION 3:
LIVING FREE

Learning to Live Free

Several years ago, I tore my rotator cuff. Despite attempts to rehabilitate it with physical therapy, it was clear that I needed surgery. The surgery was successful, but to recover the functional use of my arm, I had to go to physical therapy for several months.

In many ways, the path I took to regain the use of my shoulder is very much like the path we take to stay free of wounds. Getting free often happens when we encounter God in the midst of our brokenness. My testimony of overcoming rejection highlights that there are times when we need more than simply a good Bible study. I am not in any way minimizing the importance of Bible study. It is vital to our Christian walk and emotional health. However, we must not make the study of God's Word an end in itself. The truths in the Bible are to be experienced. Without learning and applying the truth of God's Word, we will not be able to maintain our freedom.

The truths in the Bible are to be experienced.

A lack of understanding of how to maintain and live in freedom has caused people to lose their freedom. The Bible says, "My people are destroyed for lack of knowledge" (Hosea 4:6). Kenneth Hagin noted that more people lose their healing over a counterattack than any other way. The gospel of Luke recounts the story of Jesus being tempted in the wilderness by the devil. When the temptation in the wilderness was over, the devil "left him until an opportune time" (Luke 4:13). Leon Morris writes, "There is no freedom from temptation in this life. There was not for Jesus, and there is not for us."[122] Satan hates your freedom. And while we should never live in fear of him, it is wrong to treat him as if he doesn't exist. The Bible tells us that we are "not to be ignorant of his schemes" (2 Cor 2:11).

To stay free, we first must continue practicing those things that brought us freedom. We live in a fallen world amongst fallen people. Everyone gets slimed at some time. As a result, there will be events in our lives where we will need to forgive those who have offended us. We will need to continue identifying the lies we believe and replacing them with the truth. We will continue to ensure that we haven't opened any doors to the enemy and close them if necessary.

In addition to continuing to practice what produced freedom, there are things we can do to help make us wound resistant. These are hearing from God, sowing and reaping, and having a strong identity. We will look at these truths in this section.

---

[122] Leon Morris. *Luke: An Introduction and Commentary*, Tyndale New Testament Commentaries (Downers Grove, IL: InterVarsity Press).

HEARING FROM GOD

Several years ago, I went through a very difficult time with a group of people who were extremely antagonistic, brutal in the way they spoke to me. I can still remember them calling me on the phone just to tell me how worthless I was. I am convinced that if I was in a lineup with Adolf Hitler and you asked them who the nicer one was, they would have picked Hitler. Their verbal abuse was far beyond anything I had ever heard. I remember getting off the phone and telling Joanie about it. Her response was simply, "It's from the devil." I replied, "That may be true, but I need more than that." I was struggling with what they said. I was trying to extract what was true in their comments from what was not. My mindset was that they had to be partially correct, and if I was somewhat to blame for the situation, I wanted to learn from it. I went off alone to hear from the Lord. He took me to the gospel of John, where Jesus is rebuking the Pharisees and says,

> You are of your father the devil, and you want to carry out your father's desires. He was a murderer from the beginning and does not stand in the truth, because there is no truth in him. When he tells a lie, he speaks from his own nature, because he is a liar and the father of lies. (John 8:44)

The Lord spoke to me and said, "There is no truth in him. Not partial truth, no truth." He then said something I will never forget, "Geoff, you will never find the truth sifting through lies." As soon as I heard those words. I was free. I immediately stopped analyzing what they said and dismissed it as an attack on my character.

You will never find
the truth sifting through lies.

I had been walking with the Lord for over thirty years when this occurred. I had heard thousands of messages, read hundreds of books, had taught the Word thousands of times. Yet I had never heard the simple statement that the Lord spoke to me that day. If I had to rely on what I had heard in the past, I wouldn't have received the instant freedom that occurred when the Lord simply said, "Geoff, you will never find the truth sifting through lies."

Walking in freedom requires hearing from God. Books, sermons, and conferences are all good, but it was never God's plan that everything we need comes through other people. God desires to have an ongoing relationship with each of his children. Hearing from God is key to walking in freedom.

God desires to speak to us

The first and most important truth to understand is that God desires to speak to his children. In Jeremiah, God invites us into his counsel, "Call to me and I will answer you and tell you great and unsearchable things you do not know" (Jer 33:3 NIV). It is our Father's desire to know him and his ways. In Colossians, Paul prays,

> We are asking that you may be filled with the knowledge his will in all wisdom and spiritual understanding, so that you may walk worthy of the Lord, fully pleasing to him: bearing fruit in every good work and growing in the knowledge of God. (Col 1:9,10)

In Ephesians, Paul prays a similar sentiment,

> I pray that the God of our Lord Jesus Christ, the glorious Father, would give you the Spirit of wisdom and revelation in the knowledge of him. I pray that the eyes of your heart may be enlightened so that you may know what is the hope

of his calling, what is the wealth of his glorious inheritance in the saints, and what is the immeasurable greatness of his power toward us who believe, according to the mighty working of his strength. (Eph 1:17-19)

God is not trying to hide from us. His desire is that his children would know him and his ways. Often when Jesus would teach, he would say, "Let anyone who has ears listen" (Matt 11:15, Mark 4:9, Mark 4:23, Luke 14:35), or "Take care how you listen" (Luke 8:18). Jesus ends each of the seven letters to the seven churches in Revelation with the statement, "Let anyone who has ears to hear listen to what the Spirit says to the churches" (Rev 2:7, 2:11, 2:17, 2:29, 3:6, 3:13, 3:22). Hearing is vital to having an ongoing relationship with God.

IMPORTANCE OF HEARING

"So faith comes from hearing, and hearing by the word of Christ" (Rom 10:17 NASB).

The Christian life is a life of faith (2 Cor 5:7). Without it, we cannot please God (Heb 11:6). This makes faith of paramount importance. So how does faith come? It comes by hearing. Without the Word, there can be no hearing, and without hearing, there can be no faith. Pleasing God requires walking by faith which requires hearing.

The Word of God is not solely the written Word, even though the written Word is of paramount importance. Anytime God speaks to us, whether through the Bible, prophecy, the indwelling Holy Spirit, dreams, or visions, what he speaks is his word to us.

To grow and mature as Christians, we must develop the hearing ear. Newborn babies receive nourishment from their mother's milk, food their mother has already digested. Similarly, new believers often receive much of their spiritual nourishment and instruction from others around them. Maturity requires us to learn to hear from God for ourselves, to stay connected to him.

DEVELOPING THE HEARING EAR

Learning to hear begins with recognizing that we are designed by God to hear. Hearing God is not a special gift reserved for super spiritual saints. Everyone who has accepted Jesus as Lord can hear.

God has designed his children to be able to hear him. For years I wondered if I was hearing him or if it was just my imagination. Jesus said, "My sheep hear my voice, I know them, and they follow me" (John 10:27). After reading that verse, I decided to accept what Jesus said. I am one of his sheep, and therefore I know his voice. He also said, "They will never follow a stranger; instead they will run away from him, because they don't know the voice of strangers" (John 10:5). So not only do I know his voice, I will not be led astray by the voices of others. I continued to meditate on those verses and accepted them as true. The more I focused on this truth, the more I heard his voice.

The Bible declares, "For we are his workmanship, created in Christ Jesus for good works, which God prepared beforehand, that we should walk in them" (Eph 2:10). We are his workmanship. God has made each of us. We are handcrafted by the creator. Everything he has called us to do has already been built into our spiritual DNA. We can hear his voice because he made us to hear. Hearing is a heart issue. Any child of God who truly desires to hear will hear what God is saying.

Any child of God who truly desires to hear will hear what God is saying.

Get in the Word

If we want to develop the hearing ear, we need to spend time in the Word of God, the Bible. God sounds like his book. He is not double-minded. He is not going to say one thing in his Word and speak something contradictory to our hearts. Spending time in his Word calibrates us to his voice. The more we learn to hear him in his Word, the more readily we will be able to hear him as he speaks to us in other ways.

Get Quiet

Blaise Pascal, the famous French mathematician, philosopher, and theologian, said, "All of humanity's problems stem from man's inability to sit quietly in a room alone." The psalmist says, "Be still and know that I am God" (Ps 46:10 NIV). In 1 Kings 19, we have the story of Elijah running away from Jezebel. The Lord tells him to stand on a mountain.

> God tells Elijah, "Go out and stand on the mountain in the LORD's presence." At that moment, the LORD passed by. A great and mighty wind was tearing at the mountains and was shattering cliffs before the LORD, but the LORD was not in the wind. After the wind there was an earthquake, but the LORD was not in the earthquake. After the earthquake there was a fire, but the LORD was not in the fire. And after the fire there was a voice, a soft whisper. (1 Kings 19:11-12)

God was not in the wind, the earthquake, or the fire. He was in the soft whisper. Kenneth Hagin has said, "Many people are looking for the spectacular and missing the supernatural that is right there all the time."[123] If we want to hear from God, we need to get quiet.

---

[123] Kenneth E. Hagin, *How You Can Be Led by the Spirit of God*, Second Edition, Faith Library Publications (Tulsa, OK: K. Hagin Ministries, 1989), 34.

King Hezekiah was facing a crisis. The prophet Isaiah had just told him that he was going to die. In response, "Hezekiah turned his face to the wall and prayed to the LORD" (Isa 38:2). He got rid of all distractions, determined to hear from God. The more we learn to get quiet, the more we will hear his voice.

Importance of Humility

"Therefore, as the Holy Spirit says: Today, if you hear his voice, do not harden your hearts as in the rebellion, on the day of testing in the wilderness" (Heb 3:7,8). Hearing God's voice should lead to obedience. Hearing without obedience leads to self-deception (James 1:22). Continued failure to obey the voice of God leads to a hardened heart which keeps us from hearing. It is essential to not take the Word of God as a suggestion, something to be considered and potentially discarded. One of the best ways to keep a tender heart is to quickly obey and repent when needed.

PRACTICE

"But solid food is for the mature, for those who have their powers of discernment trained by constant practice to distinguish good from evil" (Heb 5:14 ESV). Hearing God is a skill that can be developed by practice. As we continue to spend time in his presence, listening to him, we hone our ability to hear him. Practice implies that there will be mistakes. Don't get discouraged. Mistakes are not synonymous with failure. Continue to listen and obey, and your spiritual senses will be sharpened to hear him.[124]

---

[124] For more in depth teaching on this subject, I recommend, Mark Virkler, *4 Keys to Hearing God's Voice*, Destiny Image Publishers (Shippensburg, PA, 2010).

Sowing and Reaping

"In the beginning, God created the heavens and the earth" (Gen 1:1).

Creation was not haphazard. God created plant life, trees, and all vegetation, before placing the animals on earth. If he had done it the other way around, we could have ended up with a rhinoceros on top of a tree. Not a pretty sight. There is order to our world. The earth rotates on its axis once every twenty-four hours. Every 365.25 days, the earth completes a lap around the sun.

There are laws and principles that govern our world. The most obvious one is gravity. Sir Isaac Newton did not invent or discover gravity. It was here all along. What he did was define it, quantify how it works. And because of that, if someone drops an object, knowing how far it is falling, they can calculate how long it will take to reach the ground and how fast it is going at each stage of its descent. Through research, study, and experimentation, science has in many cases developed an understanding as to how natural laws such as gravity work. Engineers then use these principles to develop machinery and equipment that improves our lives. Everything from cars to airplanes to cell phones, blood pressure monitors, and titanium golf clubs (a true, life-changing breakthrough) is the result of engineers applying scientific principles. It is the reliability, the certainty of these principles, coupled with our knowledge of how they work, that allows us to harness these principles for productive good.

On December 17, 1903, the Wright brothers were the first to fly a motor driven, heavier than air aircraft successfully. The principles governing air flight have existed since the beginning of time. However, it took until 1903 for mankind to develop a sufficient understanding of these principles and how to apply them to harness them successfully with the world's first airplane flight.

These principles work whether someone likes them or not. If they were to say, "I don't believe in gravity," it wouldn't stop gravity from operating. These principles work because God created them. It is mankind's responsibility to learn, apply, and benefit from them.

Just as there are principles that govern our physical world, there are principles that govern the unseen world, the world of the spirit. I am not advocating formulaic, push-button Christianity. I am not suggesting that we use God to get what we want. I am saying that just as there are principles in the physical world, there are principles in the unseen, spiritual world. To believe otherwise would be to conclude that the material world was formed out of a more chaotic spiritual world. The God who created the seen world also made the unseen world. Just as there is God ordained order to the seen world, there is a God ordained order to the unseen world.

As previously stated, our understanding of these physical principles is the result of study, research, observation, and experimentation. The scientific method is based on observation involving empirical data (data that is sensory, unbiased, and replicable), from which conclusions are derived.

While the scientific method is of great help in discovering physical principles, it is of little benefit in identifying spiritual realities. The kingdom of God is unseen. It does not come with outward show even though it is in our midst (Luke 17:20,21). We can't physically see the kingdom of God, the world of the spirit, angels, or demons. As a result, the scientific method is of little value in learning spiritual truths. So, what do we do? If the spiritual world where God dwells is real (which it is), and if we are citizens of this unseen kingdom (which we are if Jesus is our Lord), then how do we learn about it? How do we navigate through it, given that our senses are not designed to detect spiritual realities? The answer is simple yet profound. God has given us his Word and the Holy Spirit to teach us and guide us into his truth. The Word of God is our window into the spiritual realm so that we may understand God and his ways (Isaiah 55).

God is a spirit (John 4:24). We are spirit beings (1 Thess 5:23). As a result, what we do has spiritual consequences whether we realize it or not. The spirit world has dominion over the natural world. It is the prevailing realm. Scriptures state that "the universe was created by the word of God so that what is seen was made from things that are not visible" (Heb 11:3). The physical world was created by the non-physical, spiritual world.

God, in his sovereignty, has seen fit to establish the world (seen and unseen) on certain principles that he has revealed to us so that we can use them for productive good. As human beings, we are in a unique position in that we live in both realms (the spiritual and the physical). What we do in this physical world has consequences in the unseen, spiritual world, and vice versa.

One issue within the Body of Christ is that some people have little regard for God's Word and his principles. Failure to accept these principles doesn't negate or lessen their operation. For example, gravity works whether someone believes in it or not. If someone who didn't believe in gravity were to jump off a building, they would fall to the earth. Their opinion about gravity would have no effect on the outcome. When we disregard natural or spiritual principles, they typically work against us due to our careless misuse of them. The principles that God has established on the earth, both in the seen realm and the unseen realm, are working twenty-four hours a day, seven days a week.

PRINCIPLE OF SOWING AND REAPING

One of the most pervasive principles revealed in the Bible is sowing and reaping. The principle of sowing and reaping is first revealed as part of the creation account in Genesis:

> Then God said, "Let the earth produce vegetation: seed-bearing plants and fruit trees on the earth bearing fruit with seed in it according to their kinds." And it was so. The earth produced vegetation: seed-bearing plants according to their kinds and trees bearing fruit with seed in it according to their kinds. And God saw that it was good. (Gen 1:11,12)

Notice that everything reproduces according to its kind. Apple seeds produce apples, and orange seeds produce oranges.

God reestablishes the principle of sowing and reaping after the flood, where he says, "As long as the earth endures, seedtime and harvest, cold and heat, summer and winter, and day and night will not cease" (Gen 8:22). Notice he says, "as long as the earth endures." So as long as we are here on earth, seedtime and harvest (another way of saying sowing and reaping) will exist.

The principle of sowing and reaping does not just work in the physical world, the seen realm. In Mark, Jesus makes the following statement:

> The kingdom of God is like this, he said. A man scatters seed on the ground. He sleeps and rises night and day; the seed sprouts and grows, although he doesn't know how. The soil produces a crop by itself—first the blade, then the head, and then the full grain on the head. (Mark 4:26-28)

Not only does sowing and reaping work with vegetation, but Jesus also says that sowing and reaping is how the kingdom of God operates. Sowing and reaping works with vegetation because it is first and foremost, a principle of the kingdom. The seed sprouts and grows even though the man who sowed doesn't know how. It operates because it is a principle of the kingdom established by God.

In Mark 4, Jesus teaches the parable of the sower. "Then he said to them, "Don't you understand this parable? How then will you understand all of the parables?" (Mark 4:13). In other words, this is the mother of all parables. This is the lynchpin. Sowing and reaping is a governing principle in the kingdom of God.

Paul also writes about sowing and reaping. In 2 Corinthians, Paul writes to the Corinthian church about an offering. In the letter, he writes, "The point is this: The person who sows sparingly will also reap sparingly, and the person who sows generously will also reap generously" (2 Cor 8:6).

In Galatians, he again discusses sowing and reaping when he says,

> Don't be deceived: God is not mocked. For whatever a person sows he will also reap, because the one who sows to his flesh will reap destruction from the flesh, but the one who sows to the Spirit will reap eternal life from the Spirit. Let us not get tired of doing good, for we will reap at the proper time if we don't give up. (Gal 6:7-9)

What is amazing is that he says, "whatever a person sows." Sowing and reaping is not just limited to offerings or vegetation; it is a governing principle that applies to everything. Like gravity, it works twenty-four hours a day, seven days a week. Like gravity, we don't get to decide when it is operational. It is working all the time whether someone wants it to or not. It is a straightforward principle: we reap what we sow. If you don't like what you are reaping, the way to change it is clear – change what you are sowing.

We see this principle at work all throughout the Word of God. In the gospel of John, Jesus is speaking with Nicodemus, and he says, "Flesh gives birth to flesh, but the Spirit gives birth to spirit" (John 3:6 NIV). In other words, when someone sows to the flesh, they reap flesh. When you sow to the spirit, you reap spirit. Sowing love, peace, kindness, and generosity is sowing to the spirit. Sowing selfishness, unforgiveness, and bitterness are all examples of sowing to the flesh.

The Apostle Paul contrasts the difference between the works of the flesh and the fruit of the Spirit:

> The acts of the flesh are obvious: sexual immorality, impurity and debauchery; idolatry and witchcraft; hatred, discord, jealousy, fits of rage, selfish ambition, dissensions, factions and envy; drunkenness, orgies, and the like. I warn you, as I did before, that those who live like this will not inherit the kingdom of God. But the fruit of the Spirit is love, joy, peace, forbearance, kindness, goodness, faithfulness, gentleness and self-control. Against such things there is no law. (Gal 5:19-23 NIV)

While this is not an exhaustive list, it helps to identify the difference between sowing to the flesh and sowing to the spirit.

Many of the Proverbs are specific applications of the principle of sowing and reaping. "If anyone returns evil for good, evil will never depart from his house" (Prov 17:13). In other words, if you sow evil, you will reap evil. "One person gives freely, yet gains more; another withholds what is right, only to become poor. A generous person will be enriched, and the one who gives a drink of water will receive water" (Prov 11:24,25).

It is essential to understand that everything we say and do is a seed. Sowing and reaping doesn't just operate when we are praying or when we are giving. It is working all the time.

Understanding sowing and reaping is vital for someone to get and stay free. I have observed many times when someone was mistreated. Rather than forgiving the offending party, they dwelled on the offense, which led to bitterness. In that fruit of bitterness is the seed of more bitterness (Gen 1:11). The offended person would then sow from that bitterness, resulting in a harvest of more bitterness. This would start a cycle of sowing and reaping to their own destruction. Often it becomes such a habit that people don't even realize what they are doing. For lasting freedom to come, the person must repent of their bitterness, forgive the offending party and begin to sow to the spirit by responding in love. This is one reason why forgiveness is so important.

***It is essential to understand
that everything we say and do is a seed.***

Years ago, a woman came to me for prayer. She had been in an abusive relationship and wanted to be free. She understood that she needed to forgive but had difficulty forgiving her abusive former boyfriend. While ministering to her, I told her to bless her boyfriend by praying and asking God to bless him, to prosper him. Whenever he came to mind, she was to speak love, blessing, and peace over him. I explained that God wanted her free, and if she could bless her boyfriend despite his actions, he no longer controlled her. I told her to do this by faith, meaning that she should bless him whether she felt like it or not. She spent the next week blessing him and was set free. She was reaping a harvest of blessing simply because she sowed blessing rather than bitterness.

God, by his spirit, is always leading us to sow to the spirit so that we will reap blessings. On the other hand, the enemy is constantly pushing, prodding us to sow to the flesh seeds of bitterness, unforgiveness, fear, and hopelessness. If he can get us to do this, we will sow to our own destruction. However, if we refuse to respond to him and sow to the spirit, we will reap a harvest that he is powerless to stop.

Satan cannot stop your harvest, so he tries to have you sow to your own hurt. He often does this by reminding us of past hurts and offenses to get us to sow to the flesh. He is powerless to stop you from being blessed if you refuse to respond to him and continue to sow to the spirit. What this means is that what other people have done to you, no matter how bad, does not determine your destiny. If you have been wronged, you still can sow good seed in response. You can sow the seeds of forgiveness, of love. What you sow in response to what they have done to you determines your destiny. The Spirit of God can free us from these past hurts, but we must continue cooperating with him by sowing to the spirit.

Every trial is an opportunity to sow to the spirit and reap victory. James 1:2 says, "Consider it pure joy, my brothers and sisters, whenever you face trials of many kinds." Why? - because in so doing, you are sowing the seeds of your own deliverance.

Regardless of how others treat us, we always have an opportunity to sow to the spirit, which results in a harvest of blessings. The faithfulness of God is that as we sow, he assumes responsibility for the how and the when of the harvest.

It's important to remember that while we reap what we sow, we won't necessarily reap where we sow. It's not unusual for someone to spend time loving someone, caring for them, only to have the person not reciprocate. Over the years, I have had people respond to my kindness by slandering me. When that happens, we must remember the admonition to "not get tired of doing good for we will reap at the proper time if we don't give up" (Gal 6:9). Someone's failure to respond appropriately doesn't stop the harvest. It just means that you will likely reap from another place.

Earlier in this book, I discussed the importance of encounters with God in achieving freedom. Gideon and the woman at the well are two examples of this. I have seen God set people free from years of abuse, years of bondage in one encounter, one inner healing session. However, if these people who had the encounter desire to stay free, they must learn to sow love, forgiveness, and blessing. We must live in harmony with God and his ways to live in freedom.

IDENTITY

DEATH BY METRICS

I spent thirty years working for an aerospace division of a Fortune 500 company. One of my positions was that of Supply Chain Manager. Like many companies, there were specific color-coded metrics (you can think of them as goals or targets) that we were measured against. If you were at or above the target, you were green. If you were in danger of falling below the target, you were yellow. If you were below the target, you were red. Red was bad and to be avoided. Eventually, we got rid of yellow simply because they didn't want people to think you were okay with not being green. After all, yellow was for wimps. You were green, or you were red. Every week, the other managers in the building would congregate at your board to review your metrics. If you were red, you needed a good reason and a suitable corrective action plan. If there was a lot of red on your board, you were in for a bad day.

This was not something unique to my company. I remember one Sunday, a woman at church brought her husband up for prayer. He was in a similar position at a large company in a different industry. She asked for prayer because the stress of his job was significantly affecting him. I asked him what was going on, and he blurted out, "everything is red." I knew what he meant and understood what he was going through. I remember praying that he would go from red to green. Kermit the frog was right. It isn't easy being green.

This may seem trivial, almost comical, but if you weren't green, the stress of staying red could weigh you down. After a while, your mood largely depended on the color of your charts. Green, you were happy. Red, you were stressed. On top of that, every year, they made the target more challenging (we called it raising the bar). If you had a good year, you had to do better the following year, or once again, you were red. In 1927, Babe Ruth set the major league record by hitting 60 home runs, a record that stood until 1961. He hit more home runs than some entire teams. If Babe Ruth had worked for my company, 1927 would have been the last year he was green, a fact I reminded my boss about, much to his chagrin.

When I look back, this was not a healthy way to live. Anyone could look at your graphs (they were all publicly displayed) and therefore determine your value as an employee based on how much green or red you had. In fact, my company standardized the graphs across all 120 divisions worldwide. That way, you could walk into any site and instantly know who was red and who was green. There was no place to hide your redness. Eventually, it was hard to not believe that your value was whatever the graphs said.

As crazy as this sounds, many of us live our lives in a similar fashion. We may not have well defined metrics (Can you imagine living like that? Hi, honey, your vacuuming is green, but your lawn maintenance is red. How well do you think that would work?), but we have categorized our value from when we were young. From a young age, we knew who were the strong kids, the fast kids, from the playground. Within the classroom, it quickly became apparent who was smart, who was artistic, and who wasn't. As we grew older, we knew who the popular kids were, who the good-looking ones were, etc. If you were on the high school football team, you were cool. If you were on the tennis team (as I was), you were not cool. The specifics changed from school to school, but the principle remains intact.

I accepted Jesus as my Savior and Lord between my junior and senior years in college. Until then, I was your typical college student. In my fraternity, one of the ways we measured our manhood was based on how quickly we could chug a beer. We had regular contests (we drank a lot of beer). Once again, you knew where you stood. It may have been a nonsensical way of determining your worth, but it was a standard many of us aspired to.

Behind all this is a fundamental need to feel good about ourselves. We need to know we are okay, that we have value, that we matter, and that somehow we measure up, even if it's to a ridiculous standard like drinking beer. As we age, it surfaces in the need to reach a certain financial status and stature in the workplace (the corner office). In ministry, this often means having a large church or some other numeric standard that indicates we've made it. Many of us spend our lives trying to achieve success. And when we get there, we realize that someone has always attained more. It's like being on a treadmill. No matter how fast or how far you run, you never really get anywhere.

**We need to know we are okay,
that we have value, that we matter.**

So, what's the answer? For years I tried to achieve significance. That sounded far nobler than success, but it has the same pitfalls. How do you measure it? And once you get there (wherever "there" is), you have to work to stay there. And while you are trying to get "there," are you insignificant? Jesus spent 30 of his 33 years (91%) preparing for ministry. If stepping into ministry, stepping into your calling, is where you achieve significance, then Jesus was insignificant for 91% of his life. Clearly, that can't be right.

The whole thing is wearying. Anything you achieve through your own effort has to be maintained by your effort. Too often, we end up looking over our shoulder to see who or what is coming up from behind us to supplant us from our position. This leads to fear and suspicion. There is no rest or peace when we live life this way.

At the core of this is an identity issue; who we are and how we obtain our value. Measuring our success and significance by any human standard means we are determining our worth by something other than what God says. This begs the question: what is a healthy biblical identity, and how does it operate in our lives?

In the world, behavior drives identity. We are defined by what we do. I'm a teacher, a fireman, etc. Our identity and our worth are works based. Who we are and how important we are is a function of what we do. Our desire to know how well we measure up to everyone causes us to develop our own set of metrics. It can be based on how much money we earn, how big a house we have, and what college we attended. If we have families, our value can often be a function of our children's success. Parents whose children attend Ivy League schools are more successful than those who attend community college. It's all achievement based. We are back in college, ranking ourselves according to our beer drinking skills with different metrics. We are back on the treadmill, expending lots of energy but never getting anywhere.

Our value in the kingdom of God is not based on our performance. Instead, it is based on what Jesus has done. Identity is the impetus for behavior. Our identity as a child of God is determined by our union with him. I'm a son, a daughter of God. I'm a new creation in him (2 Cor 5:17). I'm more than a conqueror through him (Rom 8:37). Who we are is who we are in him and because of him. We are who we are because of whose we are. Our identity can be in what we achieved or what Jesus has done for us. If it is in what we have achieved, then we are only as good as our last performance. We are constantly under pressure to perform. If we fail, then we are a failure. Basing our identity on our performance will never bring peace.

The alternative is to base our identity on who God says we are. Our standing with God and our value is all based on what Jesus did for us. And since it is based on what he did, not on what we do, our identity doesn't change with our performance. Good days, bad days, we are still his children. Basing our identity on what he says means our metrics are always green.

This sounds good, but most of us were not raised like this. To accept God's truth of who we are, we are going to have to shed the old performance-based value system. We must realize that God and God alone determines our value. When we allow what God says to be the basis for our identity, we are on stable ground.

We identify with Christ. We were crucified with him (Gal 2:20). We died with him (Rom 6:8). We were buried with him (Rom 6:4). And we were raised with him and seated with him in heavenly places in Christ (Col 3:1, Eph 2:6). Everything Jesus did, he did for us. And as we identify with him in his death, burial and resurrection, we are transformed. That is who God says I am. And if God said it, that is the way it is.

I've often felt that many of us are double-minded regarding identity. We know who we are in Christ. We can quote the verses, but it's like there are two of us. There is our in Christ identity, and then there is this other identity that is who we think we really are. And we go back and forth between the two, which produces instability in our lives. James 1:8 tells us that a "double-minded man is unstable in all his ways."

The reality is that you are who God says you are and that any other identity is a lie. You are not defined by your mistakes. You are not defined by what others think of you. You are not defined by how much red or green you have on your charts. You are not the sum total of your achievements. You are not your dysfunction.

So how do we resolve the two conflicting identities? Often, we try to reconcile the two. This doesn't work. You can't reconcile light and darkness. Truth and lies don't mix. Freedom comes from knowing who we are in him and letting that define us. That requires us to reject any conflicting identity.

The first step is realizing that we are who he says we are, which is non-negotiable. James 1:22 tells us that the Word is a mirror. When I look in a mirror, I see who I am. I may not like what I see, but the mirror doesn't lie. We must accept what God says even when it doesn't feel genuine.

The reality is that you are who God says you are and that any other identity is a lie.

That same passage (James 1:22-25) tells us that the hearers of the Word see who they are in the mirror, but then they go their way and forget who they are. This is where the identity double-mindedness sets in. We hear what God says we are, but then we forget and let other things define us. However, the doer of the Word stays in the Word and continues to meditate on it until their life reflects what they see from the mirror of God's Word. Doing the Word under the New Covenant is largely an identity issue. Doing the Word is primarily living out who you are in him, who you really are.

Years ago, I was talking to a friend of mine at church. I mentioned how God has declared us righteous. The Bible states, "For our sake he made him to be sin who knew no sin, so that in him we might become the righteousness of God" (2 Cor 5:21). It tells us that we, "have been justified" (1 Cor 6:11). To be justified is to be declared righteous.

My friend's response was, "I know what it says, but you really aren't righteous."

"The Bible says I'm righteous."

"I know what it says. God treats you as if you are righteous, but you really aren't."

"If the Bible says I'm righteous, then why am I not righteous?"

"Geoff, I know the Bible says you are righteous, but I know you. You really can't consider yourself as righteous."

My last response was, "Let me get this straight. God says I'm righteous. You say I'm not, and you want me to agree with you?" With that, my friend walked away.

The answer to our identity is simply, what does God say about it? Faith is a response to what God says. Faith agrees with what God says regardless of what it looks like. The faith response is to accept what God says as true and act accordingly. I may not look righteous, and there may be times when I don't act righteous, but that doesn't change what God said.

> *Faith agrees with what God says*
> *regardless of what it looks like.*

A word of caution here. I'm not advocating sloppy living. I'm not saying we can act anyway we want because God says we are righteous. The truth of God's Word should produce a change in our lives. The apostle Paul said,

> Therefore, my beloved, as you have always obeyed, so now, not only as in my presence but much more in my absence, work out your own salvation with fear and trembling, for it is God who works in you, both to will and to work for his good pleasure. (Phil 2:12,13)

We are to work out, to demonstrate the truth that God works in our hearts and minds. This is similar to what James says when he writes that "faith without works is dead" (James 2:17). If we truly believe what God says, we will act in accordance with that truth. If your actions never line up with the truth, then you are not acting in Bible faith. It's just mental agreement.

Paul addresses this in Romans 6,

> What then? Are we to sin because we are not under law but under grace? By no means! Do you not know that if you present yourselves to anyone as obedient slaves, you are slaves of the one whom you obey, either of sin, which leads to death, or of obedience, which leads to righteousness? (Rom 6:15,16)

Paul is not saying that obedience makes us righteous. He is saying that if we want to enjoy the fruits of righteousness, we must obey what God says. God has declared us righteous. It is up to us to live our lives demonstrating that righteousness. This is the obedience Paul is talking about. It is having our lifestyle line up with the truth God has placed in our hearts.

So how do we walk this out? The first step is meditation.

> This book of instruction must not depart from your mouth; you are to meditate on it day and night so that you may carefully observe everything written in it. For then you will prosper and succeed in whatever you do. (Josh 1:8)

You are to mediate day and night so that you can do (carefully observe) what is written. Meditation is the step that gets us from hearing to doing.

We see a similar passage in Psalm 1:

> How happy is the one who does not walk in the advice of the wicked or stand in the pathway with sinners or sit in the company of mockers! Instead, his delight is in the

Lord's instruction, and he meditates on it day and night. He is like a tree planted beside flowing streams that bears its fruit in its season, and its leaf does not wither. Whatever he does prospers. (Ps 1:1-3)

The man or woman who meditates on the Word is like a tree planted (the NASB says firmly planted). This tree is a fruit bearing tree. The fruit we bear is the byproduct of living our lives based on who God says we are.

Meditation is more than just hearing. It is pondering the truth, rolling it over and over in our minds. To meditate on the Word means to chew on it. As you meditate on the Word, the truth of the Word gets into your heart, and when the Word gets into your heart, faith is there. And when we respond to the Word in faith, God is faithful to do what he promised.

Meditating on the Word and allowing it to go into our hearts takes time. As we continue to meditate on the Word, our hearts and minds are aligned with God's will. If we are to walk in freedom, this is not optional.

Therefore, brothers and sisters, in view of the mercies of God, I urge you to present your bodies as a living sacrifice, holy and pleasing to God; this is your true worship. Do not be conformed to this age, but be transformed by the renewing of your mind, so that you may discern what is the good, pleasing, and perfect will of God. (Rom 12:1,2)

Paul is writing to Christians in Rome, admonishing them to not conform to this age but to be transformed. His writing proves that it is possible to be a Christian but still conform to this world's patterns. For us to be transformed, we must renew our minds. If we want to be transformed, we must change our thinking. The reason for this is simple. The wisdom of this world is at odds with the wisdom of God. If we are to walk as men and women of God, we must have our minds renewed to the truth of his kingdom. Otherwise, we will continue to walk based on the wisdom of this world.

So how do we do that? We start with his Word. There are over one hundred Scriptures that talk about who we are in Christ. They use phrases such as "in Christ," "in him," and "in whom." These Scriptures tell us who we are as his beloved children. As we spend time in his Word, meditating on these truths, we are looking at the mirror of his Word, which tells us who we really are. The more we meditate on these truths, the more we understand who we are. Then, when faced with a situation, we will respond based on who God says we are and not on who the world says we are.

These are life-changing truths. 1 John 4:4 says, "You are from God, little children, and you have conquered (or overcome) them, because the one who is in you is greater than the one who is in the world." When I face a daunting situation, I remind myself that the Greater One lives in me. I face problems knowing that I am not alone, knowing that the one who is in me is greater than anything I face. I have meditated on this truth until it has changed how I see myself. I no longer see myself as a victim but as a victor in Christ. It takes time to do this, but the result is a transformed life.

This doesn't happen overnight. Spiritual truths have to be practiced the same as any other skill. "But solid food is for the mature, for those who have their powers of discernment trained by constant practice to distinguish good from evil" (Heb 5:14 ESV). There is a training effect to walking with God the same way you train yourself to learn a language or sport. G.K. Chesterton said, "if a thing is worth doing, it is worth doing badly." He is not advocating being sloppy. He is saying that doing something badly is the pathway to doing it well. We need to continue to practice any skill if we desire to improve. The truths of God's Word need to be meditated on and practiced. You will make mistakes along the way, but God is well able to make up for our human failings.

BASIC TRUTHS ABOUT WHO WE ARE

We are New Creatures in Christ

"Therefore, if anyone is in Christ, he is a new creation; the old has passed away, and see, the new has come!" (2 Cor 5:17). When you accepted Jesus as Lord and Savior, you became a new creation. The old person is dead, buried. The new person is alive to God. You are not the person you were; you have been made new, washed, and cleansed by the blood of Jesus.

There is no need to try to make amends for the life you used to live. That was all settled at the cross. Any guilt, any shame from your past, has been obliterated, washed away by the blood of Jesus. There is no need to revisit your past.

We Have been Justified (made Righteous)

> He made the one who did not know sin to be sin for us, so that in him we might become the righteousness of God. (2 Cor 5:21)

> Don't you know that the unrighteous will not inherit God's kingdom? Do not be deceived: No sexually immoral people, idolaters, adulterers, or males who have sex with males, no thieves, greedy people, drunkards, verbally abusive people, or swindlers will inherit God's kingdom. And some of you used to be like this. But you were washed, you were sanctified, you were justified in the name of the Lord Jesus Christ and by the Spirit of our God. (1 Cor 6:9-11)

First Corinthians 6:9-11 describes what people were before they became believers. They were sexually immoral, drunkards. But now they are no longer those things. Now they have been washed by the blood of Jesus. They have been sanctified (set apart) and justified (made righteous).

"If by the one man's trespass, death reigned through that one man, how much more will those who receive the overflow of grace and the gift of righteousness reign in life through the one man, Jesus Christ" (Rom 5:17). Romans 5 contrasts the fall of man with the cross. Five times in the chapter it uses the term "much more" establishing that what Jesus accomplished on the cross was much more than what happened in the fall. Verse 17 clearly states that we have received the gift of righteousness. This is not something we earned. It is not something we deserve. It is something that was given to us as a free gift. I didn't earn it, and I don't have to work to keep it. Righteousness (right standing with God, being right with God) is given to us as a gift. We are now declared righteous based on what Jesus has done. Striving to be right with God is a thing of the past.

We are God's Children

See what great love the Father has given us that we should be called God's children—and we are! The reason the world does not know us is that it didn't know him. Dear friends, we are God's children now, and what we will be has not yet been revealed. We know that when he appears, we will be like him because we will see him as he is. And everyone who has this hope in him purifies himself just as he is pure. (1 John 3:1-3)

The Father loves us so much that we are now his children. We are heirs of God and joint heirs with Jesus (Rom 8:17). "For you did not receive a spirit of slavery to fall back into fear. Instead, you received the Spirit of adoption, by whom we cry out, 'Abba, Father!'" (Rom 8:15). We have been adopted into his family with full rights and privileges. We can call the almighty God, creator of heaven and earth, Abba, which means daddy. This is not a term that servants were allowed to use. This is a term reserved for members of the family. We are now part of his family, not because of what we did but because of what Jesus did. God once again has the family he so desired back in the garden of Eden. We are not orphans. We are not on the outside looking in. We have a seat at the table with our father.

We are not orphans....
We have a seat at the table
with our father.

We Qualify

Giving thanks to the Father, who has qualified you to share in the inheritance of the saints in light. He has delivered us from the domain of darkness and transferred us to the kingdom of his beloved Son, in whom we have redemption, the forgiveness of sins. (Col 1:12-14 ESV)

God has an inheritance, and we automatically qualify to share in it. What did we have to do to qualify? Absolutely nothing. We didn't even qualify on our own. He qualified us. And because he qualified us, there is nothing we can do to disqualify ourselves.

Every year the Indianapolis 500 is run on Memorial Day weekend. It is an automobile race that has been run since 1911. It is one of the biggest events in auto racing. During the month of May, teams compete to qualify to race in the event. Only thirty-three cars qualify.

What you may not know is that it is the car, not the driver, who qualifies for the race. If a driver is unavailable, his team can have someone else qualify the car. On race day, the driver gets to drive in the race even though he didn't qualify. Someone else qualified for him, and he reaps the benefit. In the same way, we qualify to share in the inheritance of God's children despite doing nothing to warrant qualification. Jesus went to the cross, took our sins, and rose again, and in so doing, he qualified us for all eternity. The Bible says that all of God's promises are "Yes", and "Amen" (2 Cor 1:20). They are all ours because of what Jesus did.

We are the Temple of the Holy Spirit

In the wilderness, God instructed the children of Israel to build the tabernacle as a place where he would dwell (Exodus 25). The tabernacle was to go where the children of Israel went. Once a year, on the day of atonement, the high priest could enter the most holy place and make atonement for the people's sins (Leviticus 16). You didn't treat this in a cavalier manner. Aaron's sons presented unauthorized fire (meaning they didn't do it according to God's instructions) and were struck dead (Lev 10:1-3). Despite being the high priest, Aaron was told that he couldn't enter the most holy place whenever he desired (Lev 16:1,2).

The presence of God is holy, sacred, and not something to be treated as common. In 2 Samuel 6, David and his men are bringing the ark of God back. Rather than having the priests carry it on poles, as God instructed, they take it back on a cart. During the trip, the oxen carrying the cart stumble. Uzzah reaches out to keep the ark from falling. This was probably just an instinctive move to protect it. The Bible tells us that God "struck him dead on the spot for his irreverence" (2 Sa 6:7). While this seems strange, it highlights the incompatibility between sinful flesh and the holiness of God.

During Solomon's reign, God had his people construct the temple. It took thirteen years to complete it. During the dedication of the temple, the Bible tells us, "When the priests came out of the holy place, the cloud filled the Lord's temple, and because of the cloud, the priests were not able to continue ministering, for the glory of the Lord filled the temple" (1 Kings 8:10,11).

What I find amazing is that under the New Covenant, the blood of Jesus has so cleansed us that we are now the temple of the Holy Spirit (1 Cor 6:19). Instead of being struck dead by encountering God's presence, we carry it with us. This means that wherever I go, God goes. It is impossible for me to go to a "God forsaken place," for wherever I go, he goes. Once I get there, the place can't be God forsaken because he lives in me and goes wherever I go.

This is not just a theory; it is a living reality. The Holy Spirit is in me, going wherever I go, leading, and guiding me. I don't have to go to a special place to meet with God; he's right inside of me. I never pray for God to be with me because he has promised to "never leave you or forsake you" (Heb 13:5). I'm never alone. I'm never without him. He is always right there inside of me. We house the very presence of God. Why is this? I believe one of the reasons is so that we can minister his presence wherever we go.

We are the People of God

But you are a chosen race, a royal priesthood, a holy nation, a people for his possession, so that you may proclaim the praises of the one who called you out of darkness into his marvelous light. Once you were not a people, but now you are God's people; you had not received mercy, but now you have received mercy. (1 Pet 2:9,10)

We have been chosen. We are his people. We are a holy nation. We are the people of God. We have received mercy. He desires that we proclaim his praises. This is not a promise for the hereafter. It is a present tense reality. This is not something we have to work to achieve. It is who we are right now as his sons and daughters. We are not striving to become this. We are living in the reality of this. We are God's people. I belong to him. He is my father. I am his son.

People often talk about inheriting traits from their parents. There is an old saying that "The apple doesn't fall far from the tree." While that is true, it is incredibly freeing to identify father God as my father. I am Geoff Wattoff, son of George and Marion Wattoff. But it is far more transformative to recognize that I am Geoff Wattoff, son of the Most High God. As I identify with my heavenly father, I become more and more like him.

Walking this Out

> Therefore, my dear friends, just as you have always obeyed, so now, not only in my presence but even more in my absence, work out your own salvation with fear and trembling. For it is God who is working in you both to will and to work according to his good purpose. (Phil 2:12,13)

God works on the inside of us, changing us, and helping us to renew our minds. As we do this, we are to respond to these truths with fear and trembling. Fear and trembling is "an Old Testament expression (see Ps 2:11; Isa 19:16) denoting humble reverence, dependence, and devotion to God."[125] This passage is analogous to James 1:22-25 which talks about the mirror of God's Word.

For this to be fruitful in our lives, there are two practices we must employ. The first is to spend time in his presence, in his Word, not just reading but meditating on the truths presented there. As we do that, the Holy Spirit takes those words and reveals the truth of who God is and who we are. As we allow those words to penetrate our hearts and renew our minds, we are transformed (Rom 12:2). Faith regarding these truths comes into our hearts (Rom 10:17).

---

[125] Loh, I-Jin, and Eugene Albert Nida. 1995. *A Handbook on Paul's Letter to the Philippians*, UBS Handbook Series. New York: United Bible Societies.

The second practice is to begin to apply these truths in our daily lives. This is what it means to be a "doer of the Word" (James 1:22-25). As we learn to live these truths, we see their manifestation in our lives and those to whom we minister. This is not a complicated process, but it does require diligence. This is not something we can do occasionally or haphazardly. But as we employ these two practices consistently, they produce fruit consistently (Ps 1:1-3).

Being Comfortable in
Your Own Skin

Many years ago, I was ministering to a woman who was raised in an abusive household. Her father was an alcoholic who would get violent when he was drinking. It was a situation where no one in the home felt safe. Her recollections of this went back to when she was a child in her crib.

This woman had become a Christian, and despite being a godly woman, she was still plagued by her past. As I ministered to her, God set her free from this bondage. When the session ended, she looked at me and said, "I don't know who I am. I don't have an identity." Her identity had been stolen at such a young age that even though she was now free from the abuse, she didn't know who she was. Now that she was free, she could begin understanding her identity based on who God said she was.

In John 11, Jesus raises Lazarus from the dead. Lazarus comes out of the grave alive but still bound hand and foot (v. 43). Jesus then commands those around him to unwrap Lazarus. While he is no longer dead, he is still constrained by the grave clothes, looking and smelling like a dead man. His movement is hampered. For Lazarus to walk free, he must be separated from his grave clothes. He would then need to bathe to be rid of the smell. While being raised from the dead was an event, becoming separate from the clothes and smell of death was a process.

Similarly, understanding who we are is both an event and a process. When we accept Jesus as Lord, we are transferred from the kingdom of darkness into the kingdom of God (Col 1:13). We are new creatures in Christ (2 Cor 5:17), declared righteous (2 Cor

5:21). All of these things happen when we accept Jesus as Lord. However, understanding who we are, what it means to be a child of God, and learning to walk as his beloved children is a lifelong process.

When we talk about identity, we talk about who God says you are. It is who you really are. Only when we embrace who God says we are can we be truly free and live authentic lives. Shame, guilt, and the mindset that we are not good enough, that we don't measure up, are all lies designed to keep us from fully being who we really are. The fear of being rejected for being different, not being like everyone else, keeps us from ever truly embracing our God given uniqueness.

I spent many years in a manufacturing environment. One of the goals of manufacturing is to limit the variability of the manufacturing process. The Japanese are the best at this. They excel in designing things that are manufacturable. They minimize the number of parts required to assemble a unit. If you look at car bumpers, not only do the Japanese design the bumper with fewer parts, they use fewer types of fasteners. This helps control inventory, simplifies the supply chain, and makes it less likely that someone will use the wrong fastener, reducing the possibility of manufacturing defects. This is one reason their products tend to be the most reliable. I could go on and on with this (I'm sure you're enthralled), but I think my point is clear that in manufacturing, variability is bad.

We make a mistake when we apply this line of reasoning to people. In society, a certain amount of aggregation is necessary. Clothing stores lump sizes into small, medium, and large. (I used to be small, grew into medium, and if I don't stop eating ice cream, I will continue to transition into large. But I digress.) None of us fit these sizes perfectly, but the alternative is for everything to be custom fit which is expensive and impractical. So, a certain amount of aggregation makes our lives more convenient.

We do a disservice when we apply this concept to each of us in the body of Christ. The goal is not for us to be interchangeable parts. It is to help men and women in their pursuit of intimacy with God and, through that intimacy, to fulfill their destiny. And because we are all different, this is in many ways, a singular journey. While I am not against discipleship classes, at best, they provide a foundation for growth. They are a means to an end, not the end. Aggregation, while convenient, forces us to ignore what makes us unique. It causes us to miss what is beautiful about each and every one of us.

Maybe a better, albeit imperfect, analogy for discipleship would be the college experience. My freshman year, I sat in a large lecture hall with over a hundred other students listening to physics lectures. By my senior year, I was in classes of twelve to twenty students. My senior design project was in teams of three. While I was one of many students graduating with an Industrial Engineering degree that June, no two of us had the exact same path.

Two hundred years ago, Eli Whitney developed the concept of interchangeable parts. Without it, modern manufacturing would be impossible. However, in the Body of Christ, there are no interchangeable parts. There are individuals, all uniquely handcrafted by the ultimate creator. I have a friend who is an expert on dream interpretation. If I desire to speak to him and he is unavailable, I never think, "I'll just talk to another dream guy." What makes my friend amazing is so much more than his gift. It's the sum total of who he is. And while others have similar skills, there is only one like him. While many people have similar skills to each of us, there is only one you, only one me.

When I was young, my mom would buy flavored straws. There were chocolate, vanilla, and strawberry flavored straws. They were probably vile tasting, but as a kid, I loved them. You would drink your milk through these straws, and the milk would take on the flavor of the straw. I think that at our best, we are like flavored straws. The Holy Spirit that lives in you is the same as the Holy Spirit that lives in me. But when you speak to and minister to someone, it will not sound the same as when I do it. My speech, at its best, is the wisdom of the Holy Spirit through the flavored straw that we call Geoff. The same holds true for all of us.

I wondered why God would do this. He could have made us all the same flavor so that it sounded the same no matter which vessel he was using. The truth is that our individual traits actually enhance the flavor of the Holy Spirit through us. In God's kingdom, uniqueness is not a problem to be managed. Rather it is to be embraced, celebrated, and encouraged. Dr. Mike Hutchings writes, "I believe the greatest expression of shalom—of wholeness—is when we can be our authentic selves."[126]

One of the challenges with this approach is that we can't stamp out men and women of God the way we stamp out manufactured parts. If you study church history, most of the great men and women we revere were not cookie cutter Christians. They embraced who they were and what they were called to do, even in the face of significant opposition. Robert Frost said, "You cannot succeed by being like everybody else. The opposite of success is not failure but conformity. You must be willing to take the lonely road."

The previous section focused on understanding our identity in Christ, who God says we are. As important as this is, there is another layer of identity, who we are as individuals. God made each of us unique, and we need to not only accept but celebrate our

---

[126] Mike Hutchings. *Supernatural Freedom from the Captivity of Trauma*, (Shippensburg, PA: Destiny Image Publishers), 48.

uniqueness. Part of accepting our unique identity is learning to be comfortable with whom God has made us, which some call being comfortable in your own skin.

The Bible tells us that we "have been remarkably and wondrously made" (Ps 139:14). Ephesians 2:10 tells us that we are "his workmanship." One translation says we are his masterpiece. We all know this on an intellectual level, but despite that, many of us spend years trying to measure up, trying to prove to ourselves and others that we are not failures.

Many of us measure ourselves to a standard. If we match up well, we are okay. If we don't, the response is all too often to work harder and become more like someone else. That standard is almost always based on what other people have achieved and may have nothing to do with who God made you or what you are called to do. If we go down that road, working harder toward an artificial standard will take us farther from our God ordained uniqueness. As long as the goal is based on the acceptance of others, we will struggle to live as our authentic selves. We are like a jigsaw puzzle piece - if we try to be like someone else, we change the shape of the piece and won't fit where God intended. The only way to fit is to be the person God intended us to be.

I love the church, but I have been in churches where people mean well but don't help us accept who God made us. Sometimes, they try to force someone into a role based on what is needed rather than based on who they are.[127] Using the idea that we are body parts (see 1 Corinthians 12), let's say you are a hand. You go to church, and you are looking to serve. You are a hand, but the

---

[127] I need to clarify this statement. If you are new to a church, the leadership doesn't know you and it is prudent for them to want to get to know you, to find out if you are faithful before putting you in a leadership or ministry position. Don't expect to walk in and be recognized as a prophet, teacher, or leader without first proving that you are a faithful servant. Being a faithful servant is part of who you are. They are not being unfair. They are using wisdom.

church is looking for a foot. They look at you and conclude that you are kind of like a foot. You have five fingers; a foot has five toes. There is a left and a right hand, just as there is a left and a right foot. The hand and the foot are both connected to joints - the hand is joined to the arm via the wrist and the foot to the leg via the ankle. So, they ask you to be a foot.

Not wanting to disappoint, you agree and start serving as a foot. Of course, you are not a foot; you are a hand. You are trying your best. It quickly becomes apparent that you are struggling, and your ankle and leg are struggling to work with you. Finally, the church sends you away to a conference, "How to be the Foot God Created You to be."

You go, and the conference room is filled with feet. They are all laughing, telling foot stories, and having a good time. It quickly becomes apparent that you are not one of them. They look different, and you are the only one who thinks they smell funny (after all, they are feet). Surprisingly, no one but you notice the smell. Your observation is quickly processed by others as having a bad attitude. They are all telling stories, but you are struggling. Try as you might, you are failing at being a foot.

You go back to church and try your best to suck it up and be a good foot. But you continue to struggle, and your attitude starts to go south (something apparent to everyone). Eventually, a foot joins the church. They then replace you with the foot, which is reveling at being attached to the ankle. Everyone concludes that you didn't try enough and had a bad attitude.

This may seem ridiculous, but it will ring true for more people than we like to admit. I believe in serving, but contrary to what some believe, we are not interchangeable parts. I'm an introvert, meaning I find greeting folks at the door of a church before service painful. Extroverts don't seem to understand why greeting is hard for me. It's just being friendly. Aren't we all called to love one another and be hospitable? We are, and while I love people and spending time with them, my strength is not in greeting people I haven't previously met. I have a friend who was part of a church where the leadership told her that she was like a square peg in a round hole. Try as you might, a square peg doesn't fit in a round hole.

It can be frustrating when you seem to be invisible to those around you. You have a heart to do something, but no one recognizes it. I have been a member of several churches, and few, if any of them, ever thought I could teach until after they heard me. But God is faithful and knows where you live and where you fit in the body of Christ.

Many of the people in the Bible lived in relative obscurity until their appointed time arrived. Joseph spent thirteen years as a slave in Potiphar's house and in prison, seemingly forgotten. I'm sure there were times when he questioned if his dream was from God or if it would ever come to pass. But he wasn't forgotten by God, and he went from prison to prime minister of Egypt in a day. Moses spent forty years as a fugitive in Midian, a "largely barren Sinai wilderness."[128] When it was his time, God got his attention at the burning bush.

Another example is David, who was tending sheep. The prophet Samuel comes to Jesse's (David's father) house to anoint the next king. He has Jesse present all of his sons. Jesse doesn't include David. Even David's own father doesn't see him for who he is called to be. It doesn't matter. God knew where David was.

When Jesus called his twelve disciples, he knew where they were when he called them. God arrested Saul of Tarsus on the road

---

[128] Stuart, Douglas K. 2006. *Exodus. Vol. 2. The New American Commentary.* Nashville: Broadman & Holman Publishers.

to Damascus (Acts 9) and transformed him into Paul, an apostle who wrote much of the New Testament. Jonah tried to run from the call of God. God sent a fish to swallow Jonah up and spit him out onto dry land (Jonah 1). Not surprisingly, Jonah repented. The point is simply this: God knows where you are, and he knows what you are called to do. And if you are faithful where you are, he will find you and place you where you need to be.

Many years ago, I had a vision where I was playing Little League baseball. In the vision, I was about eight years old and playing center field. I was always small for my age, so in this vision, it looked like the glove went halfway up my arm, and the hat was too big for my head. I was down in the semi-crouch position that all great outfielders are in (notice I am including myself in that elite club of great outfielders). It was clear that I was taking this very seriously. After all, this was not life and death. It was far more important. It was Little League.

Just then, the batter hit the ball to deep center field. Making my best Willie Mays impression, I turned and ran back to the fence. At eight years of age, I had a better chance of the ball hitting me on the head than I did of catching it. I was back at the fence when in the vision, I saw a huge transparent hand, representing the hand of God, lift me up above the fence, and I made this amazing catch. Worthy of Willie Mays.

The scene then shifted. I'm still in center field, but no one is hitting the ball there, and I'm bored. I yell, "I want to play shortstop," and move to the infield. The problem is I'm left-handed, and you can't play shortstop well when you are left-handed. To compensate for this, I'm trying extra hard. The point is that there was grace for centerfield, but there was no grace for shortstop. Just then, the Lord spoke to me and said, "Don't be seduced by the allure of what others are doing."

For some reason, it is very easy to fall into the trap of comparing ourselves to others. When we do that, one of two things will happen. If we compare ourselves to those struggling, we tend to fall into pride. More commonly, we compare ourselves to those we feel are doing better than we are. When that happens, we feel like we are less than who God wants us to be. It is a trap because we will never be as good trying to be like them as they are simply because God didn't make us to be them. Simon Sinek, a well-known consultant, has said, "Comparison is the deadliest thing we can do to ourselves because we will always come up short. All it does is exaggerate all of our insecurities."[129]

> **"Don't be seduced by the allure of what others are doing."**

Who we are and who God called us to be should match. Why does Jesus heal? Because that is who he is. He is a healer. Why did he save us? Because he is the savior. It's in his nature. Spend time with someone who is called to teach the Bible. They love digging into the Word and discussing it with others. I have had friends tell me that I'm always teaching. Someone who is an evangelist is always looking to win the lost. It's not just what they do. It's who they are.

It has taken me years to be comfortable with being who God made me. I now not only accept who he has made me, I enjoy it. I have learned it is much easier, more peaceful, and more fruitful to be who God has made me to be. The Bible says, "We are his workmanship, created in Christ Jesus for good works" (Eph 2:10). What I am called to do and who I am called to be match. God

---

[129] Simon Sinek, (@simonsinek), "Your Most Self-Destructive Habit," Twitter, April 22, 2021, 3:02 p.m., https://twitter.com/simonsinek/status/1385323066 734022657?lang=en.

doesn't call me to do something out of sync with who he made me to be. This may sound strange, but I give you permission to be who God created you to be.

In the gospels, Jesus sends out the twelve. He then tells them:

If anyone does not welcome you or listen to your words, shake the dust off your feet when you leave that house or town. Truly I tell you, it will be more tolerable on the day of judgment for the land of Sodom and Gomorrah than for that town. (Matt 10:14,15)

If they don't receive you, that's on them, not on you. For years I felt it was somehow my fault if someone didn't welcome me or wasn't valued. That would cause me to be hyper-critical regarding everything I did. In doing this, I gave other people power over me that they never should have had. Sometimes, people would use my sense of inferiority to manipulate me. If I ever offended someone, I assumed it was my fault and had to make it right. That was no way to live. I remember God telling me, "If you were Jesus, you would have apologized to the Pharisees for offending them." The Bible says, "The fear of mankind is a snare, but the one who trusts in the Lord is protected" (Prov 29:25).

When we are insecure, we look for the approval of people. In doing that, we give them power over us that they should never have. Manipulative people use this power to control others. This is not a good way to live. So how do we get past all this? It's easy to look in the mirror and say, "I'm amazing," but that alone isn't enough.

Being an engineer, I enjoy solving problems. Solving problems involves gathering data to define the situation. That's why the pop psychology approach of simply telling everyone they were amazing without any rationale never worked for me. If you are going to believe you are amazing, you are significant; there has to be a reason for your belief. There has to be data to support it, or the statement has no solid foundation.

As a Christian, I believe that the ultimate source of all truth, all reality is God. "In the beginning, God created the heavens and the earth" (Gen 1:1). It all starts with him. "All things were created through him, and apart from him not one thing was created that has been created" (John 1:3). Moses asks God what to say to the Israelites when they ask him who sent him. God replies, "I AM WHO I AM" (Exod 14:14). God is. Everything, whether seen or unseen, has its beginning and gets its life from him. All true wisdom comes from him. He is the source of all life.

In the gospels, Thomas asks Jesus what the way is. Jesus responds with, "I am the way, the truth, and the life. No one comes to the Father except through me" (John 14:6). The way is not a method, not a creed, not a ritual, but a person. Any truth that can't be traced back to God is not truth.

Not only is Jesus the truth, but his Word is the truth. He says, "Sanctify them by the truth; your word is truth" (John 17:16). The Holy Spirit is the Spirit of truth (John 14:17). These Scriptures clearly show us where to find the truth. God is the truth - Father, Son, and Holy Spirit. His Word is the truth. If we want the truth, we know where to look.

This is critically important. If we are going to shed the lies, the false self-image many of us have labored under, we will have to have a weapon strong enough to displace it. That weapon is the sword of the spirit, the Word of God (Eph 6:17). It's vital to be established in the truth of who you are and to be comfortable with whom God made you to be.

This truth is not just an intellectual idea. It is something to be experienced. It doesn't come solely from study; it is the fruit of a relationship. It is not only possible; it is the heart of God that you experience his love in a very real, tangible way. To do this, we need both the Word of God and the Spirit of God.

This is not something I can impart to you by prayer. Instead, it is something that develops as we spend time in his presence, in his Word, listening to him speak to us. As we walk out what he tells us, we are increasingly conformed to his image (Rom 8:29). The apostle Paul tells us:

> Therefore, my dear friends, just as you have always obeyed, so now, not only in my presence but even more in my absence, work out your own salvation with fear and trembling. For it is God who is working in you both to will and to work according to his good purpose. (Phil 2:12,13)

God is working in us, renewing our minds as we spend time in his Word, speaking to our hearts as we spend time with him. We are then to work it out with fear and trembling. "Fear and trembling" is a "stereotyped Old Testament expression (see Ps 2:11; Isa 19:16) denoting humble reverence, dependence, and devotion to God."[130] We work out and act on what God has placed in our hearts.

The New Living Translation renders Phil 2:13 as, "For God is working in you, giving you the desire and the power to do what pleases him." That is astounding. God is the one who gives us not only the power but the desire to do what pleases him. He is conforming our will to his will.

> If you abide in me, and my words abide in you, ask whatever you wish, and it will be done for you. By this my Father is glorified, that you bear much fruit and so prove to be my disciples. (John 15:7,8)

---

[130] I-Jin Loh and Eugene Albert Nida, *A Handbook on Paul's Letter to the Philippians,* UBS Handbook Series (New York: United Bible Societies, 1995), 68.

I love this Scripture. It tells me it is possible to reach a place where I can ask whatever I want, and it will be done, because my will has been brought into alignment with his. This is not manipulating God. This is reaching a place in my relationship with him where my prayers reflect his will. This alignment of my will with his does not happen until I learn to abide in him and have his words abide in me. This is spending time in his presence, getting quiet, hearing his heart, and submitting my will to his until my will is conformed to his. The more I do this and act accordingly, the more I learn to live as the person God called me to be. This is what it means to live an authentic life. No longer will you live for the praise, the approval of people. You are focused on an audience of One. You are his child, and you are living as the person he created you to be.

The Role of Community

For just as the body is one and has many parts, and all the parts of that body, though many, are one body—so also is Christ. For we were all baptized by one Spirit into one body—whether Jews or Greeks, whether slaves or free— and we were all given one Spirit to drink. Indeed, the body is not one part but many. If the foot should say, "Because I'm not a hand, I don't belong to the body," it is not for that reason any less a part of the body. And if the ear should say, "Because I'm not an eye, I don't belong to the body," it is not for that reason any less a part of the body. If the whole body were an eye, where would the hearing be? If the whole body were an ear, where would the sense of smell be? But as it is, God has arranged each one of the parts in the body just as he wanted. And if they were all the same part, where would the body be? As it is, there are many parts, but one body. The eye cannot say to the hand, "I don't need you!" Or again, the head can't say to the feet, "I don't need you!" On the contrary, those parts of the body that are weaker are indispensable. And those parts of the body that we consider less honorable, we clothe these with greater honor, and our unrespectable parts are treated with greater respect, which our respectable parts do not need. Instead, God has put the body together, giving greater honor to the less honorable, so that there would be no division in the body, but that the members would have the same concern for each other. So if one member suffers, all the members suffer with it; if one member is honored, all the members rejoice with it. (1 Cor 12:12-26)

In this passage, the apostle Paul is likening us to members of a body. Collectively, we all make up the body of Christ. One is a hand, another a foot, someone is an elbow, a liver, etc. Each of us is a different body part. God designed it that way. We are designed to be different. As the Scripture passage above explains, if we were all the same, we wouldn't be a functioning body. A healthy body necessitates that we are all different parts with unique abilities and functions. While all that is true, we are connected. Each body part needs the other body parts to function. Without the legs, we cannot move from one location to another. Without the hands, we cannot hold anything. Each body part is equally important.

Rather, speaking the truth in love, we are to grow up in every way into him who is the head, into Christ, from whom the whole body, joined and held together by every joint with which it is equipped, when each part is working properly, makes the body grow so that it builds itself up in love. (Eph 4:15,16 ESV)

The body is held together at the joints. The joints are where the different body parts connect. In other words, our connections to each other are what hold us together. It is only in community that the body can function effectively.

We especially need each other when we are going through intense difficulty or when we are wounded. No doubt, you have seen someone on crutches with a broken leg. Their arms and shoulders are being used to help themselves stay mobile while the fractured leg heals. We never think about it, but the rest of the body compensates for the broken leg so that it can heal. The same thing happens when a member of the body of Christ is wounded. The rest of the body provides assistance so the injured member can heal. When we are wounded, we need to allow the rest of the body of believers to give aid and assistance so that we can recover.

**It is only in community that
the body can function effectively.**

We not only need others around us when we are wounded, but we also need others to encourage us to be who God made us to be. Many years ago, I was at seminary, hanging out with a few of my classmates. I said something, and as soon as I said it, my friend Shelli said, "But Geoff, you're so kind." Up to that point, I never considered myself kind. I knew I was a good person, but I didn't see myself as kind. I had a choice to make. I could either reject what she said or grab onto it. I knew that Shelli was a good friend, and I knew she wouldn't flatter me. I realized that she saw something in me that I didn't see. Maybe it was in an embryonic state, but it was there. I chose to accept what she said and see myself as kind.

Another time at seminary, I commented how everyone around me was an amazing man or woman of God. As soon as I said that, another friend of mine said, "Yes, and you're one of them." Up to that point, I never saw myself that way. I often struggled, feeling that I didn't measure up. Once again, I chose to accept what my friend said and embrace this truth. Now when someone pays me a compliment, I receive it as encouragement from the Lord through that person.

"For I want very much to see you, so that I may impart to you some spiritual gift to strengthen you, that is, to be mutually encouraged by each other's faith, both yours and mine" (Rom 1:11,12). Paul, the great apostle, is looking forward to fellowshipping with the saints at Rome. He is eager to impart a spiritual gift. He is also looking not only to encourage them but also to be encouraged by them. "As iron sharpens iron, so one person sharpens another" (Prov 27:17 NIV). Just as certain things in the Christian life come from our personal time with the Lord, there are also things that come as we commune with other believers. Both are necessary. It is important to spend time in the presence of like-minded believers who will call out the gold that is in you, even if you don't see it. We are members of a body. None of us can walk this walk with God in isolation. As we fellowship together, we are strengthened. I encourage you to find your tribe - fellow believers who will speak into your life, encourage you, and correct you as necessary.

EPILOGUE

You've come to the end of this book, so what's next? It's all too easy to take the book, put it on a shelf and go on to something else. Please don't do that. The principles here are to be lived out daily for the rest of our lives. Some of you have experienced great freedom as you have applied the principles in this book. Others of you may still feel like there is a way to go. God wants you free, and no matter how free you may become, more freedom is always available. Continue to walk out your freedom, day by day. If you do so, you will experience greater joy and peace than you ever imagined.

About the Author

Dr. Geoff Wattoff is an adjunct professor at Global Awakening Theological Seminary, teaching inner healing. He received his Doctor of Ministry degree in 2015 from United Theological Seminary in Dayton, Ohio.

For over forty years, Geoff has been ministering in churches, Bible schools, and small groups, bringing people into an awareness of their true identity in Christ. Along with his wife, Joanie, he has been ministering inner healing for the past ten years and has seen God set hundreds of people free from the effects of physical abuse, sexual abuse, trauma, shame, and depression.

He and his wife currently reside in Broken Arrow, OK, with their three children and three grandchildren.